Turnip Greens
Ham Hocks &

GRANNY'S BUNS

Dianne C. Evans

ABOUT THE AUTHOR:

Dianne Evans wrote her first cookbook in 1964 and was hooked!
Since then she has authored 5 more cookbooks, owned her own
bakery'/catering business, run several Plantation/Hunting
Preserve Main Houses, including Horseshoe Plantation in
Tallahassee, Florida. By special invitation, she served a southern
dinner to the Rockefeller Family in New York and catered a Long
Island luncheon for 70 members of the New York Garden Club.
She was Executive Chef in the home of Campbell Soup's CEO,
John Dorrance. She is mother of 6, grandmother of 7 and wife of
47 years.

Granny Illustrations by Cheryl Benner.
Background cover designed & drawn by Emery Evans.

Publisher:
Miss Dee's Kitchen™
P. O. Box 3332, Boone, NC 28607
Websites: www.missdee.com **or** www.grannycookbooks.com
e-mail: dianne@missdee.com
Miss Dee's Kitchen is a subsidiary of EvanCraft, Inc.

CONTENTS

Dedication:

Dedicated to 3 really great Grandmothers:

My Mother,
Shirley Cooper

My Grandmother,
Tisha Cooper

My Mother-In-Law,
Kitty Clyde Evans

Introduction

Keep the family silver. Just give me Grandma's sugar cookie recipe! This idea came from an article I read a couple of years ago by Karen Baar, (she actually said "Mom's" recipe). Sol Katz, professor of anthropology at the University of Pennsylvania said "Mention heirlooms and most of us think of jewelry, photographs, china, or other objects typically handed down from generation to generation. What we forget, sometimes until it's too late, is the value of our family recipes. I've seen people carry family recipe books that are 150 years old. They are as significant as family Bibles. When you make a family recipe, you're taking a piece of your own past, reconstructing it and connecting with times gone by."

It was for this reason that I created a family cookbook in 1999 for my 6 grown children. It included all of the recipes they grew up with, along with family photographs of their growing up years and of our grandchildren. Needless to say, they were so happy with it and proudly show it to everyone. *And* their old family favorite recipes are always at their fingertips.

I decided to write this cookbook based on the same idea using the good old "tried and true" recipes that span the 1940's to the present. You won't find fat-free cooking here! But old fashioned family-style good eating! Many are the original 1940's & 1950's recipes that are currently popular Diner favorites!

Since the theme of this granny's book is mostly 1930's, '40's and '50's, most of the photographs I've used are from those times.

I hope you find some of the old favorites that you thought were lost forever and they bring back some warm and fuzzy memories for you!

Dianne Evans

P. S. All of the children's photos (except my childhood ones) are our grandchildren.

Granny's Dinner Menus

#1

Chicken 'N' Dumplings, p. 91
Cornbread Muffins, p. 50
Easy No-Cook Banana Pudding, p. 197

#2

Mom's Roast Beef, p. 83
Roasted New Potatoes
Buttered Baby Carrots
Creamy English Peas, p. 108
Amish Potato Bread, p. 49
Pineapple Au Gratin, p. 186

#3

Swiss Steak, p. 87
Old Fashioned Mashed Potatoes
Fresh Tiny Butterbeans
Honey Bran Muffins, p. 31
Coconut Cream Pie, p. 166

#4

Mom's Meatloaf, p. 84
Macaroni & Cheese Deluxe, p. 112
Fried Green Tomatoes, p. 113
Buttermilk Skillet Cornbread, p. 51
Fudge Brownies, a la Mode, p. 204

#5

Stuffed Pork Chops, p. 102
Fried Creamed Corn, p. 110   Buttered Green Beans
Sour Cream Blueberry Muffins, p. 32
Grandma Dee's Apple Crisp, p. 195

More Delicious Menus are on pages: 46, 47, 54, & 154

Granny's Kitchen Arithmetic

HANDY SUBSTITUTIONS:

1 cup self-rising flour = 1 cup all-purpose flour plus 1 teaspoon baking powder and 1/2 teaspoon salt.

1 cup cake flour = 1 cup all purpose flour minus 2 tablespoons.

1 cup all-purpose flour = 1 cup cake flour plus 2 tablespoons.

1 teaspoon baking powder = 1/2 teaspoon cream of tartar plus 1/4 teaspoon baking soda.

1 tablespoon tapioca (for thickening) = 1-1/2 tablespoon all-purpose flour.

1 tablespoon cornstarch = 2 tablespoons flour. (for thickening)

1 cup sugar = 1 cup packed brown sugar or 2 cups sifted powdered sugar.

1 cup packed brown sugar = 1 cup granulated sugar plus 1-1/2 tablespoons molasses.

1-1/2 cups corn syrup = 1 cup sugar plus 1/2 cup water.

Corn syrup, honey and molasses are interchangeable.

Apple spice mix, 1 teaspoon = 1/2 teaspoon cinnamon, 1/4 teaspoon nutmeg, 1/8 teaspoon allspice and a dash of ginger.

Pumpkin spice mix, 1 teaspoon = 1/2 teaspoon, 1/4 teaspoon ginger, 1/8 teaspoon allspice and 1/8 teaspoon nutmeg.

Gingerbread spice mix = 3 teaspoons ginger, 1 teaspoon cinnamon and 1 teaspoon cloves.

Allspice mix, 1 teaspoon = 1/2 teaspoon cinnamon plus 1/8 teaspoon ground cloves.

1 teaspoon dry mustard = 1 tablespoon prepared mustard.

3 small eggs = 2 large eggs

1 whole egg = 2 egg yolks (for custard)

1 whole egg = 2 egg yolks plus 1 tablespoon water (for cookies)

2 whole eggs (for healthy substitution) = 2 egg whites plus 1 whole egg.

1 cup sour cream = 2/3 cup milk plus 1/3 cup butter.

1 cup buttermilk = 1 tablespoon vinegar or lemon juice plus sweet milk to equal 1 cup.

1 ounce square unsweetened chocolate = 3 tablespoons cocoa powder plus 1 tablespoon shortening or butter, melted.

1, 4 ounce package German Sweet Baking chocolate = 1/4 cup cocoa powder, 1/4 cup sugar and 1/4 cup shortening.

1 tablespoon fresh herbs = 1 teaspoon ground, crushed dry herbs.

EQUIVALENT MEASUREMENTS:

A **"dash"** = a little less than 1/8 teaspoon

3 teaspoons = 1 tablespoon or 1/2 ounce

1/8 cup = 2 tablespoons or 1 ounce

1 "jigger" = 1.5 ounce or 3 tablespoons

1/4 cup = 4 tablespoons or 2 ounces

1/3 cup = 5 tablespoons plus 1 teaspoon

1/2 cup = 8 tablespoons or 4 ounces

3/4 cup = 12 tablespoons or 6 ounces

7/8 cup = 14 tablespoons or 3/4 cup plus 2 tablespoons

1 cup = 16 tablespoons or 8 ounces

1 cup = 1/2 pint or 8 fluid ounces

1 cup flour = 4 ounces

2 cups = 1 pint or 16 ounces

4 cups = 2 pints or 1 quart or 32 ounces

4 tablespoons butter = 1/4 cup or 2 ounces or 1/2 stick

8 tablespoons butter = 1/2 cup or 4 ounces

1/2 pint (1 cup) whipping cream = 2 cups whipped

8 large egg whites = about 1 cup

12 large egg yolks = about 1 cup

5 whole large eggs = 1 cup

1/4 cup egg substitute = 1 whole large egg

WEIRD MEASUREMENTS: Reducing recipes can get pretty sticky with strange quantities. Perhaps these will help.

1/3 of 2 tablespoons = 2 teaspoons

1/2 of 1 tablespoons = 1-1/2 teaspoons

1/3 of 1/4 cup = 1 tablespoons plus 1 teaspoon

1/3 of 1/2 cup = 2 tablespoons plus 2 teaspoons
1/3 of 3/4 cup = 1/4 cup
1/2 of 1/3 cup = 2 tablespoons plus 2 teaspoons
1/2 of 3/4 cup = 6 tablespoons
2/3 cup = 10 tablespoons plus 2 teaspoons
1/2 of 1-3/4 cup = 3/4 cup plus 2 tablespoons
2 pints = 1 quart
1 quart = 4 cups
2 quarts = 1/2 gallon
4 quarts = 1 gallon
8 quarts = 1 peck
4 pecks = 1 bushel
16 ounces (dry measure) = 1 pound

Bread— 1 slice = 1/2 cup soft crumbs
Crackers—3/4 cup crushed = 1 cup bread crumbs
Saltines—28 = 1 cup fine crumbs
Chocolate wafers—19 = 1 cup crumbs
Graham crackers—14 squares—1 cup fine crumbs
Vanilla wafers—22 cookies = 1 cup finely crushed crumbs
Lemons, 1 medium = 2 to 3 tablespoons juice plus 2 teaspoons
       grated rind.
       4 to 6 lemons = 1 cup juice
Limes, 1 medium = 1-1/2 to 2 tablespoons juice plus 1-1/2 tea-
       spoons grated rind.
Oranges, 1 medium = 1/3 cup juice and 1 tablespoon grated rind.
Marshmallows,
       10 large = 1 cup
       10 miniature = 1 large marshmallow
       8 ounce package = 4-1/2 cups
Milk,
       Evaporated, 5 ounce can = 2/3 cup
           12 ounce can = 1-1/2 cups
       Sweetened condensed, 14 ounce can = 1-1/4 cups
Nuts, Almonds, 1 pound = 3-1/2 cups shelled
       Peanuts, 1 pound shelled = 3 cups

Pecans, 1 pound shelled = 4 cups

Walnuts, 1 pound shelled = 4 cups

Apples, 3 medium = 1 pound or 3 cups sliced

Cheese, 8 ounces grated = 2 cups

Cream cheese, 3 ounce package = 6 tablespoons

Coconut, 1 pound = 6 cups shredded

Elbow macaroni, 2 cups (uncooked) = 4 cups cooked

Rice, long-grain, 1 cup (uncooked) = 4 cups cooked

Grits, 1/4 cup raw = 1 cup cooked

Peaches, 2 medium = 1 cup sliced

Strawberries, 1 quart = 4 cups sliced

Sugar,

Brown, 1 pound box = 2-1/3 cups firmly packed

Confectioners, 1 pound box = 3-1/2 cups

Vegetables,

Carrots, grated, (for carrot cake), 1 pound = 3 cups

Onion, 1 medium chopped = 3/4 to 1 cup

1 tablespoon instant minced = 1 small chopped

Potatoes, 3 medium, sliced or chopped, = 1 pound or
3 cups

Yeast, 1 cake compressed yeast = 1 package active dry or
3 teaspoons

1 package active dry = 1/4 ounce or 3 teaspoons

Vanilla, 1/4 teaspoon powdered = 1 teaspoon vanilla extract

1 vanilla bean = 1 teaspoon vanilla extract

Sometimes you'll run into an old recipe that calls for a certain "#" can. Here are the average contents for those kinds of recipes:

Can Size	Cupfuls	Weight
#300	1-3/4 cups	15 ounces
#303	2 cups	16 ounces
#2	2-1/2 cups	20 ounces
#2-1/2	3-1/2 cups	28 ounces
#3	4 cups	33 ounces
#10	13 cups	106 ounces

What's for Breakfast?

RECIPES:

"Flossie" at Grandma Tisha's farm, helping with the chores. 1938

A Breakfast Memory

My most memorable breakfasts were in the late 1930's at my Grandma Tisha's farm in South Georgia.

Mama (as family members called her) had one of those wonderful old farm houses where all of the bedrooms were on one side of the house and the kitchen, dining room and living room were on the other side. A long wide hall separated the two sides. You could stand at the front screen door and look down the hall and see the well on the back porch!

Since there was no electricity, every room had a fireplace. My job, as a five-year-old with a little red wagon, was to keep the wood boxes full.

I loved staying at the farm with "Mama". We were big buddies! Her name for me was "Flossie". And sometimes she called me "Little Gal". I slept with her in her big feather bed. Each night she would heat a brick at the fireplace, wrap it up in a piece of flannel and tuck it under our covers at the foot to keep our feet warm. As we watched the fire slowly dwindle down and go out, we chatted and giggled like a couple of little girls, our feet pressed against the warm brick under mountains of handmade quilts.

The next morning, at *3 o'clock* Mama would get up and build a fire in the fireplace so I could get up to a warm room. She went into the kitchen where Aunt Judy was already at the big black iron cook stove preparing breakfast.

And what a breakfast it was!! Smokehouse sausage or smoke-cured ham with lots of red-eye gravy. Scrambled eggs, made with eggs that I had gathered the day before from the hen-house. This was all topped off with hot buttered grits, Mama's biscuits, almost as big as her fluffy feathered pillows, freshly churned butter and lots of homemade preserves. Very often we had fried squirrel or rabbit that Uncle Roy had killed. These were dressed, cleaned, cut up and fried like chicken with gravy raised over them and simmered until fork-tender. What a feast!

SMOKEHOUSE COUNTRY HAM WITH RED-EYE GRAVY

Desired number pieces of country ham
1/2 cup water
2 cups brewed coffee

Cook ham in large skillet over medium heat 5 to 7 minutes on each side until brown. Remove ham and keep warm, reserving drippings in skillet. Add the water, to the hot skillet, scrapping the pan, then add brewed coffee, about a cup or two. Simmer, stirring occasionally, until reduced by half. Pour into a little pitcher and serve with ham and hot buttered grits.

SAUSAGE GRAVY

1 pound mild bulk pork sausage
2-1/4 tablespoons all-purpose flour

1 cup milk
1/2 teaspoon pepper

Fry sausage and crumble. Remove from skillet and drain. Leave 3 tablespoons of drippings in skillet. Gradually add flour to drippings stirring to brown but do not let burn. Gradually add milk, stirring as you add to desired consistency. You may only need 3/4 cup of milk. Add black pepper and crumbled sausage. Cook till smooth and hot. Serve over split biscuits.

BROWN SUGAR BACON

1 pound bacon, room temperature
1 cup light brown sugar

Preheat oven to 300 degrees. Pat each bacon slice in brown sugar, coating well. Place individual slices on a baking sheet. Bake until bacon is done, about 30 minutes. Remove and place on paper towels to drain. It will get crispy as it cools.

Sawmill Gravy

Very much like the one served at Cracker Barrel Restaurants

1 pound bulk style breakfast sausage
1/4 cup all-purpose flour
2 cups milk
Salt and pepper to taste

In a large cast-iron skillet fry sausage, stirring constantly, to breakup and brown. Remove from pan and pour all but about 2 tablespoon fat from pan. Reduce heat to low. Add flour to pan, whisking, to cook flour, for about 5 minutes. Add milk slowly, stirring constantly, scraping bottom of pan as you stir. Cook, stirring until gravy is thickened. Salt & pepper to taste. Add cooked, crumbled sausage to gravy and serve hot over split homemade buttermilk biscuits. Makes 2-1/2 cups of gravy.

Country Cabin Sausage Quiche

1 green bell pepper, chopped
1 medium, onion thin sliced
1 pound bulk sausage
2 unbaked pie shells
2 cups Cheddar cheese, shredded
3 ounce can sliced mushrooms, drained

5 large eggs
5 oz. can evaporated milk

Preheat oven to 350 degrees. Spray a skillet with Pam and cook bell pepper and onion for 3 minutes. Crumble sausage, add to pan and brown until no longer pink, about 3 to 5 minutes; drain. Divide between 2 pie shells and sprinkle top with cheese. Whisk the eggs and milk together; add drained mushroom and pour evenly over the cheese. Bake in preheated oven for 35 to 40 minutes till set. Each quiche serves 4 as an entrée or 6 as side dish.

GRITS

The standard direction for cooking grits is this:
Bring 4 cups of water to boiling, add 1 cup grits, 1 teaspoon salt
and 4 tablespoons butter. Cook on medium heat, covered, for
about 15 to 20 minutes. Stir often to prevent them from sticking to the pan. Water may be added during cooking. They should
have the consistency of oatmeal. For quick grits (not instant)
cook on medium low heat for about 10 minutes.
1 serving of grits is: 1/4 cup grits to 1 cup water & salt to taste.
Use this equivalency for the desired number of servings.

CHEESY GRITS: *Just before* taking off the stove, add grated
cheese, about 1/4 cup per 1 cup of cooked grits.

CREAMY GOURMET GRITS: Add 2 tablespoons dry chicken
broth granules and 2 tablespoons dry coffee creamer to water
when adding grits.

GARLIC GRITS CASSEROLE

1 cup quick-cooking grits	2 large eggs
1/2 cup butter	Milk, about 1/2 cup
1 (6 ounce) roll garlic cheese	Saltine cracker crumbs

Cook grits in 4 cups of water & 1 teaspoon of salt. Add butter
and cheese, stirring until butter and cheese are melted. Beat
eggs and add enough milk to make one cup liquid. Mix all together
with grits and pour into a greased 9 x 13 inch baking dish. Sprinkle with cracker crumbs and bake at 350 degrees for 40 to 45
minutes. Makes 8 servings.

CORNED BEEF HASH WITH POACHED EGGS

Preheat oven to 350 degrees. Spread **2 cans of corned beef hash** evenly into a greased 9 x 13 inch baking dish. Bake for 30 minutes or until crusty and brown on top. Meanwhile poach **6 to 8 eggs.** When ready to serve, place poached eggs on top and serve with cheesy grits and hot breakfast biscuits (p. 27). *NOTE: You can serve scrambled eggs instead of poached, if you prefer.*

FRIED APPLES

1/4 cup butter	1 cup light brown sugar
5 large cooking apples	1 teaspoon cinnamon
1/2 cup apple juice	1/4 teaspoon ground ginger

Heat butter in large skillet over medium heat. Peel and core apples and cut into 1/2 inch slices. Fry apples in butter, a few at a time, turning once till golden brown. Add more butter if necessary. Add the apple juice, sugar, cinnamon and ginger. Cover and cook over medium heat until apples are just tender and glazed, about 15 minutes. Serve with cream or if a dessert, with Cool Whip. Makes 4 to 6 servings.

Grandma
surprised a fox
In her hen house!

SUNDAY MORNING PANCAKES

2 cups all-purpose flour
4 teaspoons baking powder
1 teaspoon salt
1 cup sugar

2 large eggs, lightly beaten
2 cups milk
1/4 cup vegetable oil
1 tablespoon vanilla

Sift the flour, baking powder, salt and sugar together. In a separate bowl, combine the eggs, milk, oil and vanilla. Stir the two mixtures together, stirring just until moistened. Heat skillet to medium (350 degrees, if using an electric skillet). Add 1 to 2 tablespoons of oil in pan. Use 1/4 cup measure for each 5 inch pancake. Makes 16, 5 inch pancakes.
Note: If you use a Teflon lined pan, do not oil skillet.
APPLE PANCAKES: Peel and chop fine 1 large yellow Delicious apple and stir into the batter just before baking.

SOUR CREAM BLUEBERRY PANCAKES

2 cups milk
2 large eggs
1/2 cup sour cream
2 cups all-purpose flour
2 tablespoons baking powder

2 tablespoons brown sugar
1/2 teaspoon salt
4 tablespoons butter
1-1/2 cups fresh blueberries

Combine the milk, eggs, and sour cream together, beating well. Mix the flour, baking powder, brown sugar and salt together. Add to the egg mixture, beating just until the lumps disappear. Melt butter, adding to batter; fold in the blueberries. Pour about 1/4 cup batter on greased skillet. Makes about 12, 5 inch pancakes.

GREAT BREAKFAST ACCOMPIANMENTS:
Homemade apple butter, sautéed apples, honey, fig preserves, assorted jams, and syrups, cut-up fresh fruit and, always REAL butter.

DOLLAR PANCAKES WITH BLUEBERRY SAUCE

1 cup all-purpose flour
1 teaspoon sugar
1 tablespoon baking powder
1/2 teaspoon salt

1 large egg
3/4 cup evaporated milk
1/2 cup water
2 tablespoons soft butter

Mix dry ingredients together. Beat egg, milk and water together and add to dry ingredients. Beat well and add soft butter. (It mixes better if you melt the butter). Spoon silver dollar sized pancakes on hot griddle. Keep warm. Serve with lots of crispy fried bacon and pass the Blueberry Sauce. Serves 8.

BLUEBERRY SAUCE

Bring to a boil: **3/4 cup water and 1/4 cup sugar**
Add: **1 tablespoon lemon juice**
Mix together: **1 teaspoon cornstarch with 1 tablespoon water**
Add to syrup mixture. Cook for 1 minute, stirring constantly.
Add: **1 can blueberries, *drained*** *(or 2 cups fresh)* and cook for about 1/2 minute.

Granny's Pancake Tips:

1. Don't over beat batter. Over beating causes pancakes to be tough. Some lumps should remain.

2. To test griddle to see if it is hot enough, sprinkle a few drops of water on the hot griddle. If the drops sizzle and bounce on the surface, the griddle is ready.

3. Turn pancakes when edges are slightly dry and "bubbles" appear on top. The second side take only half as long to bake as first side.

4. Unlike waffles, you can stack pancakes in a warm oven with waxed paper between each. Set oven on lowest temperature.

5. Add finely chopped or ground pecans to pancake or waffle batter. Serve with pure maple syrup.

FARMHOUSE WAFFLES

Light & crispy! A great Sunday morning treat!

1-3/4 cups all-purpose flour	1-3/4 cups milk
1 tablespoon baking powder	1/2 cup vegetable oil
1/4 teaspoon salt	1 tablespoon vanilla
2 large egg yolks	2 large egg whites

Combine flour, baking powder and salt in a medium mixing bowl. In another bowl, beat the egg yolks slightly and stir in milk, oil and vanilla. Add egg yolk mixture all at once to dry mixture. Stir just until moistened. Beat egg whites with electric beaters till stiff peaks form and gently fold into batter. Bake according to your waffle iron's direction. Makes 12 to 16 (4 inch) waffles.

Note: If you choose not to separate the eggs, you won't get as many waffles. The beaten egg whites add to the volume of batter.
Note: I still have my 1950's waffle iron. I also seek out great old waffle irons in antique malls. I have family breakfasts with all of the waffle irons going at once!

PEACH SAUCE

2 cups fresh peaches, divided	1/4 cup water
3/4 cup sugar	Dash of nutmeg
1/4 cup lemon juice	

Bring 1 cup of the peaches, sugar, lemon juice, water and nutmeg to a boil. Reduce heat and simmer on medium low for 20 minutes. Add the other cup of peaches, stirring well. Place in a food processor and pulse *just* a couple of times. Do not puree. Spoon over waffles or pancakes. Makes 12 ounces.

GRANNY'S TIP:

Don't stack waffles, it makes them soft and soggy.. They're best served as soon as they are baked, but you can put them in a single layer in a warm oven.

GREAT-GRANDMA SCHULTZ'S FUNNEL CAKES

When I was 2 years old, I lived with Great-Grandma Schultz and Grandmother Nitz for a year in Racine, Wisconsin. Grandma Schultz's tiny bedroom was way up in the top of their house, next to where I slept. Each night after I was put to bed, I would knock softly on Grandma's door. She would let me in and we would drink Postum! On the back of the photo below is written "your Postum buddy".

Combine the following in a bowl:

1 cup all-purpose flour   **3 teaspoons sugar**
1 teaspoon baking powder   **1/8 teaspoon salt**

Gradually add:

1 large egg, slightly beaten   **1 teaspoon vanilla**
3/4 cup milk

Let mixture stand for 15 minutes. Pour oil 1 inch deep in a 12 inch skillet. Heat to 370 degrees, using a deep fat thermometer. Pour some of the batter into a large kitchen funnel, filling it 3/4 full. Holding your finger over the hole, carefully remove your finger to let the batter run out in a stream, into the hot oil, making a spiral about 6 inches in diameter. Fry till golden brown. The cakes will puff up and float to the top. Turn over, with tongs, to brown on the other side. Drain on paper towels. Sprinkle lightly with powdered sugar and eat while they're hot. Makes about six, 6 inch funnel cakes.

Great-Grandma Schultz

GRANDMOTHER NITZ'S GERMAN APPLE PANCAKE

My grandmother Nitz's name was Mathilda; she was called "Tillie".

3 large eggs	3/4 cup all purpose flour
3/4 cup milk	1/2 teaspoon salt
1/2 teaspoon vanilla	2 tablespoons butter

Preheat oven to 450 degrees. Combine the eggs, milk and vanilla; beat at medium speed with electric mixer. Mix flour and salt together and add to egg mixture, leaving a few lumps. Heat a large oven-proof skillet and add butter. Pour the batter into skillet and immediately put in hot oven. Bake for 15 minutes, then reduce heat to 350 degrees and bake about 10 more minutes until pancake is puffed and brown. Prepare apple mixture below while pancake is baking. Remove from oven and spoon apples on pancake; sprinkle with confectioners sugar. Cut in wedges.
Serves 4 for breakfast or 6 for dessert.
Optional: Top each serving with Cool Whip or whipped cream.

SAUTEED APPLE FILLING

3 tablespoons butter
2 tablespoons brown sugar
2 tablespoons white sugar
4 large Yellow Delicious Apples, peeled, cored and sliced, 1/4 inch thick.
1/2 teaspoon cinnamon

In a large skillet over medium heat, melt butter and brown sugar. Add apples, stirring and cooking till tender and brown, about 15 minutes. Stir in cinnamon.

Grandma Nitz

COUNTRY SAUSAGE CASSEROLE

1-1/2 pounds sausage
1 (2-1/2 ounce) jar sliced mushrooms, *drained*
6 slices white bread, crusts removed, cut into cubes
2 cups Cheddar cheese, grated
2-1/2 cups milk
4 large eggs, slightly beaten
1/4 teaspoon dry mustard
1 (10-3/4 ounce) can cream of mushroom soup
1/4 teaspoon grated onion
1/2 teaspoon Worcestershire sauce

Crumble and brown sausage; drain on paper towels. Combine all ingredients in a very large mixing bowl, mixing well. Pour mixture into a lightly greased 9 x 13 inch baking dish. Cover and *refrigerate overnight.* The next morning: preheat oven to 300 degrees. Bake casserole *uncovered* for 1 hour and 30 minutes. Serves 8

BREAKFAST HASH BROWN CASSEROLE

1 package (1 lb. 4 oz.) Simply Potatoes shredded hash browns,
   not frozen (found in the *refrigerator* section of the grocery store)
1 (10-3/4 ounce) can cream of chicken soup
3/4 cup sour cream
8 ounces, (1 cup) sharp cheddar cheese, grated
1/4 cup real butter, melted
2 tablespoons onion, finely chopped

Preheat oven to 350 degrees. In a large bowl combine soup, sour cream, cheese, melted butter and onion. *Mix well.* Then add hash browns and stir until well mixed. Pour into buttered baking dish. Sprinkle topping (**below**) evenly over top. Bake uncovered in pre-heated oven for 45 minutes. Serves 8 to 10
Topping: Mix together: **1/2 cup melted butter** and **2 cups Corn Flakes.**

APPLE BUTTER

4 large cooking apples (about 2 lbs.)
1 cup apple juice or apple cider
1/2 cup brown sugar, packed
1-1/2 teaspoons cinnamon

1/4 teaspoon salt
1/8 teaspoon cloves
1/8 teaspoon allspice

Combine apples and juice in a large saucepan and bring to a boil. Cover, reduce heat to simmer and cook for 25 minutes, until apples are fork-tender. Stir often. Drain apples. Put into Food Processor and pulse a few times for "chunky" style or one minute for smooth style. Return to saucepan and brown sugar, salt and spices. Cook, uncovered over medium heat until mixture is thickened, about 20 minutes, stirring often. Store in refrigerator.

FIG PRESERVES

7 pounds figs
8 cups water

6 pounds sugar
1-1/2 lemons, sliced thin

Wash figs and wipe dry. Mix the sugar and water together and bring to a rolling boil. Carefully add figs, a few at a time and cook over medium heat, stirring occasionally, until they are clear and the syrup has thickened, about 2 hours. Add lemon slices during the last 30 minutes of cooking. Pack into *hot,* sterilized jars, leaving 1/2 inch room at the top. Put a slice of lemon in each jar. (the lemon slice keeps the syrup clear) Wipe rim good and seal with *hot,* sterilized lids.
Makes about 11 to 12 pints.

GRANDMA'S BREAD BASKET

Emery & Dianne Evans
Wedding Day, Feb. 28, 1954

RECIPES:
BREAKFAST BREADS

DINNER BREADS

FRUIT & VEGGIE BREADS

BREAKFAST BREADS

BREAKFAST BISCUITS

A really good "scratch" biscuit, so light & fluffy, you'll have to butter them just to keep them from floating off the plate!

4 cups self-rising flour
1/2 teaspoon baking soda

2/3 cup shortening
(butter-flavored Crisco)
2 cups buttermilk

Preheat oven to 400 degrees. Combine flour and baking soda. Cut in shortening with pastry cutter or 2 knives. Add buttermilk and stir just until all is moistened. Turn out on a lightly floured cloth or board and gently fold the dough over in half, pat with your fingers, and repeat a couple of times. You can even "cuddle" it, cupping it with your hand around the outside edges. Pat dough down about 3/4 to 1 inch high. Using a floured glass, cut out rounds and place them in a lightly greased baking pan. Dip glass in flour each time if it gets sticky. Don't twist glass or cutter when cutting out biscuits, instead push the cutter straight down and up again. Twisting causes the edges to seal, preventing proper rising. Bake in preheated oven for 10 to 12 minutes. Makes about 16 biscuits.
Note: White Lily flour is the best flour for biscuits.

CHEESE BISCUITS: Add 1 cup grated mild Cheddar cheese to
the batter when adding buttermilk.

GARLIC-CHEESE BISCUITS: Add 1/4 to 1/2 teaspoon garlic
powder to the flour/baking soda mixture.

STRAWBERRY BUTTER: Beat together: 1 cup softened butter,
1 (10 ounce) package frozen strawberries, thawed and *drained*, and 1 cup sifted powdered sugar.

HARDEE'S BISCUITS

When we had our little "Home Sweet Home" bakery, this recipe was given to us by a lady who worked at Hardee's. This was before Hardee's home office began shipping the pre-mixed biscuit mix to their fast food restaurants. She made them every morning from scratch and shared the recipe with us! What a coo! We must have served *thousands* of these biscuits, as office workers lined up in the morning for our freshly made sausage and ham biscuits!

This is the recipe in it's original form. It can be divided.

5 lbs. White Lily self-rising flour
1 tablespoon baking powder
1-1/2 tablespoons sugar

1 lb. Crisco shortening
1/2 gallon fresh buttermilk

Preheat oven to 450 degrees. Mix dry ingredients in mixer at medium speed. Add shortening in "pieces" a little at a time until mixture looks crumbly. Add buttermilk and stir with a spoon just until dough clings together. Turn out onto a floured board and roll to one inch thick. Cut out biscuits and place on a lightly greased baking pan. Bake for 14 minutes.
This recipe will make 36, 3 inch biscuits.

*NOTE: This recipe will also make 300 **party size** biscuits to be filled with slivers of ham and turkey. For party biscuits, roll out 1/4 inch thick and cut 1-3/4 inch round. Bake at 450 degrees for 14 minutes. Serve with honey-mustard spread.*

HONEY-MUSTARD SPREAD: Combine with electric mixer: 1/2 cup butter, 1/4 cup honey and 2 teaspoons prepared mustard.
Makes 1 cup.

GRANDMA'S YEAST DONUTS

Mix the night before!

1 package active dry yeast
1 cup warm water
3/4 cup evaporated milk
1/4 cup sugar
1 teaspoon salt
1 large egg, slightly beaten
4 to 4-1/2 cups cake flour
Oil for frying

Combine yeast and water and let stand 5 minutes. Add evaporated milk, sugar, salt and egg. Add enough flour to make a soft dough. Cover and refrigerate 8 hours or overnight. Next morning, turn dough out onto a well-floured cloth and knead 5 or 6 times. Roll into a large rectangle, about 14 x 15 inches. Cut into 2-1/2 inch squares. Pour oil into a Dutch oven, about 4 inches deep. Heat to 375 degrees. Fry donuts, a few at a time, until golden. Drain on paper towels. Put sifted powdered sugar in a brown paper bag or plastic bag and add donuts, coating well with the sugar. You can use granulated sugar mixed with a little cinnamon, if you wish. Eat 'em while they're hot!
Makes about 30 donuts.

GRANDMA DEE'S CINNAMON BUNS

This was the best selling item in our little Home Sweet Home bakery. We made them *big* and they looked like little frosted feathered pillows!

1/3 cup butter, softened
1 cup hot water
1 tablespoon dry yeast
1 large egg
1/4 cup sugar
2-3/4 cups all-purpose flour
1/2 teaspoon salt

In a large mixing bowl, stir the softened butter into the hot water. When slightly cool, stir in yeast. Cover and let stand for 5 minutes. (time) With a fork, beat egg with sugar together and add to butter mixture. Stir in flour and salt. Cover tightly and refrigerate 6 hours or overnight. Dough will rise to the top of the bowl.

When ready to make rolls, **preheat oven to 375 degrees**. Punch dough down and roll out on a lightly floured board into a long rectangle, about 14 inches wide and 10 inches deep. Brush with melted butter. Sprinkle with a mixture of sugar/cinnamon.
(Ratio: 1/3 cup sugar and 2 teaspoons cinnamon)
Roll up and cut into 1 to 1-1/2 inch slices. Place in a greased pan, sides touching. Let rise till doubled, about 2 hours.
Bake in preheated oven for 25 minutes.

While still warm, brush tops with a mixture of: **1 cup sifted powdered sugar, 1 to 2 tablespoons milk and 1 teaspoon vanilla extract.** This recipe doubles nicely.

NOTE: At the bakery we used a ratio of 2 cups bread flour and 3/4 cup cake flour. The gluten of the bread flour gives it elasticity and the cake flour softness. This was the secret of our cinnamon rolls! We always used White Lily flour.

BREAKFAST TEA MUFFINS

1 cup all-purpose flour
2 tablespoons sugar
1/2 cup milk

4 tablespoons vegetable oil
1 large egg

Preheat oven to 400 degrees. Sift flour and sugar together. Add milk and oil slowly, then beat in egg. Fill greased miniature muffin tins and bake for about 15 minutes. Sprinkle powdered sugar on them after removing from the tins, while they are still hot . This recipe will make 24, one inch muffins. This is not a sweet muffin, it's more like a bread. They make a nice accompaniment to soup for lunch.

HONEY BRAN MUFFINS

1 cup whole wheat flour
1 cup Kellogg's Bran Buds
1 teaspoon baking soda
1/2 cup raisins

1/2 cup nuts, chopped
2 large eggs
1 cup honey
1 cup buttermilk

Preheat oven to 400 degrees. Mix ingredients in order given. Spray regular sized muffin tins with vegetable spray or line with paper muffin cups. Fill 2/3 full and bake for 20 minutes for regular size muffins and about 12 to 15 minutes for miniature muffins. Makes 24 regular size or 36 mini-muffins.

Granny Says:

Always let quick bread & muffins rest for 15 minutes before putting in the oven. This gives them time to "relax" and rise slightly.

Sour Cream Blueberry Muffins

2 large eggs
1/2 cup butter, melted
1 cup sugar
1 cup sour cream

2 cups all-purpose flour
1 teaspoon baking powder
1/4 teaspoon baking soda
1/2 teaspoon salt
1 cup blueberries

Preheat oven to 375 degrees. Combine eggs, butter, sugar and sour cream. Sift dry ingredients together and stir in blueberries. Fold flour/blueberry mixture into egg mixture, blending well. Spray muffin tin with non-stick spray or line with paper muffin cups. Fill cups almost full and bake for 25 minutes.
This recipe makes 12 to 15 large regular size muffins.
In our bakery, we made these in giant muffin cups. Delicious!
NOTE: The giant muffin tins and liners can be found at kitchen shops.

Fresh Apple Coffee Cake

4 cups thinly sliced apples
2 cups sugar
2 cups all-purpose flour
1-1/2 teaspoons baking soda
1 teaspoon salt
1 teaspoon cinnamon

2 large eggs
3/4 cup vegetable oil
2 teaspoons vanilla
1 cup chopped pecans or
       walnuts

Preheat oven to 350 degrees. Combine apples and sugar. Sift flour, baking soda, salt and cinnamon together; add eggs, oil and vanilla. Fold in apples/sugar and nuts. Pour in a 10 inch tube pan which has been greased, floured and bottom lined with waxed paper. Bake in preheated oven for 50 to 60 minutes. (test with a straw for doneness) Let cool completely before removing from pan. Makes 12 to 15 servings.
Optional Icing: Combine: **1/2 cup butter, 1/2 cup light brown sugar and 2 tablespoons milk** *in a saucepan. Bring to a boil and pour over cake.*

MORAVIAN SUGAR CAKE

This was given to me by a friend who grew up across the street from Winkler's Moravian Bakery. It is in an area in Winston-Salem known as "Old Salem" and is a favorite North Carolina tourist attraction. Vickie grew up to be a sales rep for the Pillsbury Company and regularly shopped in our little Home Sweet Home Bakery. I called her my "Pillsbury Dough Girl".

2 packages active dry yeast
2 teaspoons sugar
1 cup lukewarm water
1 cup sugar
1 teaspoon salt

2 large eggs
1 cup melted butter
1 cup mashed potatoes
6-1/2 to 7 cups all-purpose
    flour

Stir yeast and 2 teaspoons sugar together into the 1 cup water. Allow to stand 5 minutes. Combine the one cup sugar, salt, eggs and butter together. Add mashed potatoes and one cup of the flour, beat till smooth. Stir in yeast mixture and beat in enough flour to make a soft dough. Refrigerate overnight This is the first rising.

The next morning, grease the bottoms of two, 9 x 13 inch baking pans. Divide dough evenly between the two pans and pat down to 3/4 inch thick. Let rise 1-1/2 hours or until it rises up and is "puffy".

Preheat oven to 400 degrees. Make shallow indentions in dough with thumb, about one inch apart. Blend topping ingredients (*below*) together and spoon into indentions in dough. Sprinkle top with cream. Bake in preheated oven for 10 minutes.

TOPPING:
1 stick butter
1 pound box light brown sugar
1 teaspoon cinnamon

Note: 1 large potato will yield, 1 cup mashed.

MORAVIAN SUGAR CAKE #2

Grandma could have opened a Bed & Breakfast with this recipe!
Also, this is an easier version, using a box of hot roll mix.

1 (16 ounce) package Pillsbury Hot Roll Mix
3/4 cup hot water (about 120 degrees)
1/3 cup sugar
1/3 cup instant nonfat dry milk
1/3 cup instant mashed potato flakes
2 large eggs
1/3 cup butter, melted

Take the yeast from the package of mix and dissolve it in the hot
water. Combine *1/2* of the flour from the mix and the rest of the
above ingredients together and with an electric mixer, beat for 2
minutes at medium speed. By hand, stir in the remaining flour
from the mix. Cover and let rise in a warm draft-free place until
doubled, about 1 hour.
Stir down and place in a greased 9 x 13 in baking dish. Cover and
let rise again until doubled and "puffy", about 45 minutes.
Preheat oven to 375 degrees. With a floured thumb, make shallow indentions in dough about 1 inch apart.
Topping, below. Sprinkle the top evenly with a mixture of the brown
sugar and cinnamon; drizzle melted butter over the top, making
sure to get butter in all of the indentions. Scatter the chopped
pecans over top. Bake in preheated oven for 15 to 20 minutes.
Cut into squares. Makes 16 servings

TOPPING:
2/3 cup light brown sugar, firmly packed
1 teaspoon cinnamon.
1/2 cup melted butter
1/2 cup chopped pecans.

BLUEBERRY TEA CAKE WITH LEMON SAUCE

2 cups all-purpose flour
2 teaspoons baking powder
1/4 teaspoon salt
1 cup sugar

1/2 cup butter, softened
3/4 cup milk
1 large egg
1 cup blueberries

Preheat oven to 350 degrees. Sift together flour, baking powder, salt and sugar. Add softened butter and mix well. Add milk and beat for two minutes. Add egg and beat one minute more. Carefully stir in blueberries. Pour into a greased 8 inch square baking dish. Bake for 50 minutes. While still warm, pour Lemon Sauce (below) over top and sides. Cut into 9 squares.

LEMON SAUCE:

1/4 cup sugar
1 tablespoon cornstarch
Dash salt
1 cup water

3 tablespoons lemon juice
1 teaspoon lemon rind
1 teaspoon butter

Mix together sugar, cornstarch and salt. Stir in water and lemon juice. Add lemon rind. Cook over medium heat until thick and clear, stirring often. Remove from heat and add butter. Stir until melted and pour over cake.

Granny's Wisdom
"Rules of Life"
Be Kind
Brush Your Teeth
Clean Your Room
Call Your Grandmother!

CHERRY CRUMB CAKE

3 cups all-purpose flour
3/4 teaspoon salt
3 teaspoons baking powder
1-1/2 cups sugar

2 large eggs
1/2 cup butter
1 (21 ounce) can cherry pie
filling

Preheat oven to 350 degrees. Sift the dry ingredients together, add eggs & butter and mix until crumbly. Spread *2/3* of the mixture in a lightly greased 9 x 13 inch baking dish. Spread **one can of cherry pie filling** evenly over top. Sprinkle remaining crumbs over pie filling. Bake for 40 minutes. Cut into squares.
NOTE: You may substitute blueberry or apple pie filling instead of cherry.

CHEESE DANISH

1 (8 ounce) package cream cheese,
softened
1/2 cup sifted powdered sugar
1 large egg yolk

1 teaspoon lemon peel
2 cans crescent rolls
1 large egg white
2 tablespoons water

Preheat oven to 350 degrees. With electric mixer on low speed, beat the cream cheese, powdered sugar, egg yolk and lemon peel together. Separate crescent rolls into triangles. Divide cheese mixture between triangles, leaving a 1/4 inch border. Roll each triangle up, starting at the wide end. Place on a lightly greased cookie sheet, shaping ends around into crescents. Brush egg white, mixed with about 2 tablespoons of water, on top of each pastry. Bake in preheated oven for 15 minutes or till lightly brown. Drizzle a "string" icing over tops of cooled pastries.
String Icing: 1 cup sifted powdered sugar, 1 teaspoon almond extract and **1 tablespoon milk.** You want a thick icing so it will drizzle pretty.

SOUR CREAM COFFEE CAKE

Cream:

1 stick butter

1 cup sugar

Add:

2 eggs, one at a time

Sift together:

2 cups all-purpose flour

1 teaspoon baking soda

1 teaspoon baking powder

Add flour mixture alternately (half at a time) with:

1 cup sour cream

Stir in:

1 teaspoon vanilla extract

Pour *1/2* of the <u>batter</u> into a lightly greased 9 x 13 inch baking pan.

Cover with *1/2* of the following <u>topping</u>:

1/3 cup light brown sugar, packed

1/4 cup white sugar

1/4 cup pecans, chopped

Pour in other *1/2* of the <u>batter</u> and cover with other *1/2* of the <u>topping.</u> Bake at 325 degrees for 40 minutes. Cut into 12 squares

Kelley and her
"Beautiful Baby"
Trophy
1985

DANISH APPLE CAKE

6 cups cooking apples, sliced
1 cup sugar
1 tablespoon lemon juice
4 cups fine macaroon cookie
   crumbs, (about 1 pound)

1/2 cup butter, melted
10 ounce jar red current
     jelly (about 1 cup)

Preheat oven to 350 degrees. Combine apples, sugar and lemon juice in a saucepan and simmer for 5 minutes. Drain, discard liquid. Push apple mixture thru a strainer to sieve. Combine macaroon crumbs and butter. Lightly press 2 cups of the crumb mixture into the bottom of a 8 inch springform pan. Top with *1/2* of the apple mixture; spread with *1/2* of the jelly. Repeat layers, using 1 cup of the crumbs, then apples, then jelly. Sprinkle remaining crumbs on top, pressing down lightly. Bake in preheated oven for 40 to 45 minutes. Chill overnight. Next day, when ready to serve, remove from springform pan and garnish with whipped cream.

APPLE FRITTERS

1-1/2 cups all-purpose flour
1 tablespoon sugar
2 teaspoons baking powder
1/2 teaspoon salt
2 large eggs

2/3 cup milk
1 tablespoon oil
3 cups peeled, finely
    chopped apples
Oil for frying

Combine dry ingredients in a bowl; add eggs, milk, oil. Add apples. Stir just until moistened. Pour oil 1 inch deep in a large skillet. Drop batter by tablespoonfuls into hot oil. Cook until golden brown on each side. Drain on paper towels; then roll in powdered sugar. Makes about 3 dozen.

FRUIT & VEGGIE BREADS

GRANDMA DEE'S APPLE BREAD

1 cup all-purpose flour	2 large eggs
1 teaspoon baking soda	1-1/2 cups chopped
1/2 teaspoon salt	apples
1/2 teaspoon cinnamon	1-1/2 tablespoons
1/2 teaspoon apple pie spice	evaporated milk
1/2 cup butter	1/2 teaspoon vanilla
1 cup sugar	1 cup pecans, chopped

Preheat oven to 350 degrees. Sift together flour, baking soda, salt, cinnamon and apple pie spice. Cream butter and sugar together, scraping sides of bowl. Add eggs, beating well after each addition. *Stir* in flour mixture with a *wooden spoon.* (*t*his is important) *just* until all flour is incorporated. Then fold in chopped apples, milk, vanilla and nuts. Spoon into a greased 9 inch loaf pan, spreading evenly. Bake in preheat oven for 45 minutes. Test with a skewer . It's done when it comes out clean.

FRESH APPLE MUFFINS

2 cups all-purpose flour	1/4 cup raisins
1/2 cup sugar	1 cup peeled, finely chopped
1 tablespoon baking powder	apples
1/2 teaspoon salt	1 large egg
1/2 teaspoon cinnamon	1/2 cup butter, softened
	3/4 cup milk

Preheat oven to 400 degrees. Sift the dry ingredients together; stir in raisins and apples. Mix the egg, butter and milk together and stir into other mixture just until moistened. Pour into 12 greased muffin cups and bake in preheated oven for 20 minutes.

Apple Cheddar Bread

2 cups self-rising flour
2/3 cup sugar
1 teaspoon cinnamon
1/2 cup chopped nuts
1 cup apples, peeled & chopped
1/2 cup Cheddar cheese, grated

2 large eggs, beaten
1/2 cup butter, melted
1/4 cup milk

Preheat oven to 350 degrees. Combine flour, sugar, cinnamon, nuts, apples and cheese. Mix the eggs, butter and milk together and stir into the other mixture until well blended. Pour into a greased and floured 9 inch loaf pan. Bake in preheated oven for one hour or until tests done.

A Cooper Family Portrait—1938

Grandma Tisha (center) with ALL 9 of her children and 5 spouses. My Mother is on the far right, my Dad is standing behind her.

BANANA NUT BREAD

More like cake than bread!

1 teaspoon baking soda
4 tablespoons buttermilk
1/2 cup butter
1 cup sugar
2 large eggs
3 very ripe bananas, mashed

1 teaspoon vanilla
1-1/2 cups all-purpose
        flour
3/4 teaspoon salt
1 cup pecans, chopped

Preheat oven to 350 degrees. Dissolve baking soda in buttermilk. Cream butter and sugar together; add eggs, bananas and vanilla. Add buttermilk mixture, flour, salt and pecans and mix well. Pour into a greased and floured 9 inch loaf pan. Bake in preheated oven for 1-1/4 hours. This is the best banana bread you'll ever put in your mouth!

ORANGE TEA BREAD

2 cups all-purpose flour
1/2 cup sugar
1 teaspoon salt
1 teaspoon baking soda
1 large egg, beaten

1/4 cup vegetable shortening
1 teaspoon grated orange peel
1 teaspoon grated lemon peel
1 cup orange juice
1 cup pecans, chopped

Preheat oven to 350 degrees. Mix together flour, sugar, salt and baking soda. Melt and cool shortening. Add to dry ingredients along with beaten egg, orange peel, lemon peel, orange juice and pecans. Mix well and pour into greased and floured 9 inch loaf pan. Cover and let rest for 15 minutes. (this is important) Bake in preheated oven for 50 minutes.

 **Granny Says:**

If God had wanted me to touch my toes,
    he would have put them on my knees.

STRAWBERRY PECAN BREAD

2/3 cup sugar
1/3 cup butter
2 large eggs
3 tablespoons buttermilk
2 cups all-purpose flour

1/2 teaspoon baking soda
1 teaspoon baking powder
1/2 teaspoon salt
1/2 cup pecans, chopped
1 cup sliced strawberries (fresh
  or frozen, thawed & *drained)*

Preheat oven to 350 degrees. Cream sugar and butter; blend in eggs and buttermilk. Combine flour, baking soda, baking powder and salt; add to creamed mixture. Stir in nuts and strawberries. Pour into greased 9 inch loaf pan and let stand for 20 minutes. Bake in preheated oven for 50 to 60 minutes or until tests done.

FROSTING:

Cream: **1 cup sifted powdered sugar, 2 tablespoons melted margarine** and *enough* **strawberries and juice to spread on top of warm bread.** Sprinkle with **more chopped nuts,** if desired.

DATE-NUT BREAD

4 large eggs
1 cup sugar
2 teaspoons vanilla

1 pound dates, chopped
1 pound pecans, chopped
1 cup all-purpose flour, sifted
1/2 teaspoon salt

Preheat oven to 300 degrees. Beat eggs until very light. Add sugar and vanilla. Dredge dates and nuts with the cup of sifted flour. Fold in egg mixture. Add salt. Grease a 9 inch loaf pan and line bottom with waxed paper. Bake in preheated oven for about one hour or until tests done.

Note: The loaf will not be firm when done but gets firm after it cools.

CARROT SANDWICH BREAD

1 cup finely grated raw carrots
1 cup light brown sugar
1 teaspoon baking soda
1 tablespoon shortening, melted
1 cup boiling water
2 large eggs
1-1/2 cups sifted all-purpose flour
2-1/2 teaspoons baking powder
1 teaspoon salt
1 cup whole wheat flour
1 cup walnuts, chopped

Preheat oven to 350 degrees. Combine carrots, brown sugar, baking soda and shortening. Pour boiling water over this mixture and stir just to mix. Cool. Beat eggs with a fork and add to cooled carrot mixture. Sift together the all-purpose flour, baking powder and salt. Stir in whole wheat flour and walnuts. Pour into a greased 9 inch loaf pan. Let rest 15 minutes. Bake in preheated oven for one hour.

CARROT TEA BREAD

3/4 cup vegetable oil
1 cup sugar
2 large eggs
1-1/2 cups all-purpose flour
1 teaspoon baking soda
1 teaspoon cinnamon
1/2 teaspoon salt
1 teaspoon vanilla
1 cup grated raw carrots
1/2 cup chopped nuts

Preheat oven to 350 degrees. Mix all of the ingredients together, in order given. Pour into a greased and floured 9 inch loaf pan. Bake in preheated oven for one hour.

Garden Fresh Zucchini Bread

3 cups all-purpose flour
1 teaspoon baking soda
1 teaspoon baking powder
1 teaspoon salt
3 teaspoons cinnamon
2 cups raw zucchini, grated

3 large eggs, beaten
2 cups sugar
1 cup vegetable oil
3 teaspoons vanilla
1 cup chopped nuts

Preheat oven to 350 degrees. Mix dry ingredients together and add all the remaining ingredients. Pour ingredients evenly into 2 greased and floured 9 inch loaf pans. Bake in preheated oven for one hour.   Makes: 2 loaves.

Pineapple-Bran Bread

1-3/4 cups all-purpose flour
2 teaspoons baking powder
1/4 teaspoon baking soda
1/2 teaspoon salt
3 tablespoons butter, softened

3/4 cup sugar
2 large eggs
1 cup Raisin Bran cereal
1 cup crushed pineapple,
    undrained
Cinnamon/sugar

Preheat oven to 350 degrees. Sift together flour, baking powder, baking soda and salt. Set aside. Cream butter and sugar together. Add eggs, one at a time and beat well after each addition. Add cereal. Stir in *1/2* of the flour mixture. Stir in the undrained pineapple, then the rest of the flour mixture. Spoon into greased 9 inch loaf pan. Sprinkle top with cinnamon /sugar. Ratio: 1/2 cup sugar to 1 teaspoon cinnamon. Bake in preheated oven for one hour. Makes: 1 loaf.

Pumpkin Bread

Great to take to the office, gift-giving or to sell at Bazaars.

3 cups sugar
1 cup vegetable oil
2 cups (16 ounce can) pumpkin
3 large eggs
3 cups all-purpose flour
1 teaspoon nutmeg
1/2 teaspoon cloves

1 teaspoon cinnamon
1 teaspoon baking soda
1 teaspoon baking powder
1/2 teaspoon salt
1 cup chopped nuts
2/3 cup raisins (optional)

Preheat oven to 350 degrees. Mix the sugar and oil together. Add canned pumpkin and eggs. In a separate bowl, mix together the flour, nutmeg, cloves, cinnamon, baking soda, baking powder, salt and nuts. (and raisins, if desired) Line two 9 inch loaf pans with waxed paper. Grease and flour the sides. Pour batter evenly between to pans and bake in preheated oven for one hour. Test for doneness.
Makes: 2 loaves.

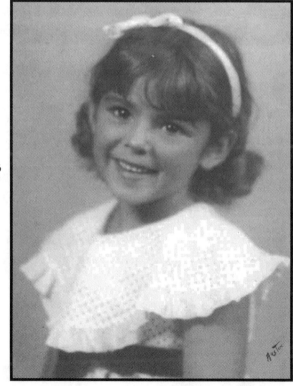

Grandma Dee,
Dianne C .Evans
1937

Grandma's Menus

LAKESIDE SUPPER
Chicken-Broccoli Casserole, p. 100
Marinated Garden Tomatoes, p. 113
French Bread & Butter
Fresh Strawberry Pie, p. 176
Iced Tea

WASH DAY BLUES
Granny uses her crock-pot on wash day.
Country-Style Beef Stew, p. 84
Breakfast Biscuits, p. 27 (cut out BIG to sop up the gravy!)
Apple Brown Betty, p. 196

FRIDAY NIGHT CHILI SUPPER
Grandma Dee's Chili, p. 57
Toppings, diced onions and grated cheese
Buttermilk Skillet Cornbread, p. 51
with lots of soft butter
Fresh Fruit Cup

PICNIC AT THE POND
Baked Sugar Cured Ham
Country Potato Salad, p. 74
Overnight Layered Salad, p. 71
Pimiento Cheese Sandwiches, p. 80
Old Fashioned Chocolate Layer Cake, p. 133
Fresh Lemonade and Iced Tea

SUMMER PORCH SUPPER

Summer Icy Gazpacho, p. 63
Shrimp & Macaroni Salad, p. 66
Breakfast Tea Muffins, p. 31
Orange Sherbet Cake, p. 135

PIG PICKIN'

Bar-B-Q Pork, p. 89
Brunswick Stew
Potato Salad, p. 74   Cole Slaw, p. 90
Hush Puppies, p. 52
Pig Pickin' Cake, p. 150

ITALIAN SPAGHETTI SUPPER

Spaghetti with Mother's Spaghetti Sauce, p. 85
Crusty Italian Bread, toasted
Strawberry Crunch, p. 187

RAINY DAY LUNCH

Emery's Seafood Gumbo, p.59
Egg Salad Sandwiches, p. 68
Four Layer Dessert, p. 189

GRANDPA'S FAVORITE BREAKFAST

Smokehouse Country Ham, p.14
Red-eye Gravy, p. 14
Cheesy Grits, p. 16   Scrambled Eggs
Hot Biscuits with Fig Preserves, p. 24

GOOD BREAKFAST MENU

Fresh Squeezed Orange Juice
Hash Brown Casserole, p. 23
Scrambled Eggs
Fried Apples, p. 17
Biscuits, p. 27 or p. 28

DINNER BREADS

ANGEL BISCUITS
They'll fly right off the plate!

1 package active dry yeast
2 tablespoons lukewarm water
5 cups White Lily plain flour
1 teaspoon baking soda
3 teaspoons baking powder

1/4 cup sugar
1 teaspoon salt
1 cup shortening
2 cups buttermilk

Preheat oven to 400 degrees. Dissolve yeast in water. Sift flour, baking soda, baking powder, sugar and salt together. Cut in shortening. Add buttermilk and last, the yeast mixture. Stir until all flour is dampened. Knead on floured board for one minute. Roll out to desired thickness and cut with biscuit cutter. *No rising is necessary.* Bake for about 12 minutes.
NOTE: Dough may be kept in refrigerator for about one week.

"A Sunday Dip in the Creek", 1949
Grandma Tisha (L) with sisters, nieces and nephew.

Yeast biscuits

2 packages active dry yeast
1/4 cup warm water
5 cups self-rising flour
1/3 cup sugar

1 teaspoon baking soda
1 cup Crisco shortening
2 cups buttermilk

Preheat oven at 425 degrees. Dissolve yeast in warm water.
Combine dry ingredients. Cut in shortening. Stir in yeast mixture
and buttermilk. Do this a little at a time, stirring carefully or
you'll run out of liquid. Mixture will be sticky. Turn out onto floured
board and cut with biscuit cutter. Unused portion will keep covered very tightly in refrigerator for one week. Bake in preheated
oven for 12 to 15 minutes. Makes about 36, 2-1/2 inch biscuits.
*NOTE: Grandma takes these to church suppers and they disap-
pear fast!*

Amish potato bread

This is wonderful! You'll swear it's Quincy's recipe!

1 package active dry yeast
1 cup lukewarm water
1 cup mashed potatoes
2 large eggs, beaten

1/2 cup shortening
1/2 cup sugar
1 teaspoon salt
3-1/2 cups plain flour

One large potato is one cup. Peel, dice and cook potato until tender. Then mash with a potato masher, Do not add any seasonings. Dissolve yeast in water. Combine with potatoes, eggs,
shortening, sugar and salt. Mix well. Add flour and blend well.
Place in lightly greased bowl and turn once to coat. Place in a
draft-free place to rise till double. (2 hours) Pat out on a floured
board and shape into rolls. Place in greased pan, sides touching,
and let rise till double. (1 hour) Bake rolls in a 400 degree oven
for about 12 minutes. For two 9 inch loaves, bake at 350 for
40-45 minutes. *Once you make this recipe, you'll use it often!*

GRANDMA DEE'S ICEBOX ROLLS

Great for holiday meals with the whole family.

1/3 cup butter, softened
1 cup hot water
1 tablespoon active dry yeast
1 large egg

1/4 cup sugar
3 cups all-purpose flour
1 teaspoon salt

Stir the softened butter into the very hot water. When slightly cool, add the yeast and let stand 5 minutes. Beat the egg and sugar together in a small bowl. Add to the yeast mixture. Stir in flour and salt. *Cover and refrigerate overnight.*
Next day; roll out on lightly floured board and cut out with 2-1/2 inch biscuit cutter or glass. Brush with melted butter and place in greased pans. Let rise till doubled, about 2 hours. Bake in pre-heated 400 degree oven for 14 minutes.
Makes about 24 rolls   Can easily be doubled or tripled!
NOTE: In our bakery we used 2-1/4 cups bread flour and 3/4 cup White Lily cake flour, but it works just fine with all-purpose flour

CORNBREAD MUFFINS

1-1/4 cups plain cornmeal
1 cup all-purpose flour
1/3 cup light brown sugar, packed
1/3 cup granulated sugar
1 teaspoon baking soda

1/2 teaspoon salt
1 large egg
1 cup buttermilk
3/4 cup corn oil

Preheat oven to 425 degrees. Combine cornmeal, flour, sugars, baking soda and salt; set aside. In a separate bowl, combine egg, buttermilk and corn oil. Stir into dry ingredients. Fill greased muffin tins or paper lined cups 3/4 full. Let rest 10 minutes. Bake in preheated oven for 15 to 20 minutes. Makes 12, 2-1/2 inch muffins *or* 6 jumbo muffins. (jumbo pans found at kitchen shop)
NOTE: A chopped apple is a good addition to cornbread batter!

BUTTERMILK SKILLET CORNBREAD

1 large egg, lightly beaten
2 cups buttermilk
1-1/2 cups self-rising
    cornmeal

1 cup self-rising flour
1 tablespoon sugar
1/4 cup vegetable oil

Preheat oven to 400 degrees. Grease a 9 or 10 inch iron skillet and place in hot oven. Mix the egg and buttermilk together; add cornmeal, flour and sugar, mixing well. Pour oil into cornmeal mixture last, mixing well. This next step is important. Pour batter into *hot* skillet. This is what gives it a nice crusty bottom. Bake about 20 to 25 minutes. Cut into wedges and serve with lots of real butter.

NOTE: A good variation : add shredded ham or crumbled bacon to cornbread batter before baking.

OATMEAL QUICK BREAD

1-1/2 cups boiling water
1 cup quick-cooking oats
1/2 cup butter, softened
1 cup granulated sugar
1 cup light brown sugar
2 large eggs

1 teaspoon vanilla
1-3/4 cups all-purpose flour
1 teaspoon baking soda
1/2 teaspoon salt
1 teaspoon cinnamon
1 cup raisins (optional)

Preheat oven to 350 degrees. Pour boiling water over oats; set aside. Cream butter and sugars together, beating well. Add eggs, one at a time, beating well after each addition. Add vanilla. Sift flour, baking soda, salt and cinnamon together and add to creamed mixture. Stir in oat mixture. Stir in "plumped" raisins, (see p. 121, Granny's Tip) Pour into a well greased and floured 9 inch loaf pan, let rest 15 minutes, then bake for 1 hour or until tests done. Let cool in pan 10 minutes, then remove and cool on wire cake rack. Makes 1 loaf.

GRANDMA DEE'S HUSH PUPPIES

1 cup self-rising cornmeal
1 cup self-rising flour
1 small onion, chopped

1 large egg, lightly beaten
Buttermilk

Heat at least 1 inch of oil in deep skillet. After frying fish, turn heat down to medium so hush puppies won't burn before they are done inside. Mix cornmeal, flour, onion and egg together. Add buttermilk, a little at a time. You don't want the batter to be "soupy" but not dry either. Drop by teaspoonfuls into hot oil. Dip spoon into glass of water each time so batter won't stick to spoon. Hush puppies will usually turn themselves over when they brown on one side.

NOTE: To make hush puppies for 3 or 4 people, use 1/2 cup self-rising cornmeal and 1/2 cup self-rising flour. The egg and onion will stay the same.

MOTHER'S HOECAKE

My mother could make the *best* hoecake! After almost 50 married years of cooking, I can almost rival hers. A lot of people use self-rising flour or add baking powder to the batter. The "secret" of *true* southern hoecake is flat, like a fritter, with no leavening. You need a black cast-iron griddle. It has no sides and needs to be very hot. You grease it, preferably with bacon grease *each* time before pouring the batter. The goal is to have very, very "lacy" edges. To accomplish this, the batter needs to be very thin.

Warning: the lacy edges won't make it to the table!

RECIPE:
2 cups plain cornmeal
1/2 teaspoon salt

Very hot water, enough to make
a thin batter

Drop about 1/2 cup of batter onto a very hot, greasy skillet. Don't be tempted to "fiddle" with it. After about 2 minutes, lift one edge to see if it's brown; turn it over and brown the other side. about 1/2 minute. Serve hot with greens, fried green tomatoes, chili, etc.

BURP BREAD

In the 1970's this recipe was extremely popular as a result of the introduction of the new Tupperware® "Fix-N-Mix" bowl. It was a very large green mixing bowl with their patented "burp" lid. To "burp", you simply lifted the rim while pushing down on the top to create a slight vacuum seal.

9 cups all-purpose flour
1-1/2 cups milk, scalded
1-1/2 cups warm water
2 pkg. active dry yeast,
    (2 tablespoons)

4 large eggs, slightly
    beaten
2/3 cup sugar
2 teaspoons salt
1 cup margarine, melted

Before you start, be sure all ingredients are room temperature. This is important for the rising process. Be sure eggs are at room temperature. Pour all of the flour into the "Fix-N-Mix" bowl and make a "well" in the center. In a *separate* bowl, combine the 1-1/2 cups of warm water, about 1/2 of the scalded milk and dissolve the yeast in it. (a whisk is good for this) Then add the rest of the scalded milk, eggs, sugar and salt to yeast mixture (*not the margarine*). Mix well. Pour all of this into the well in the center of the flour. DO NOT STIR. Seal, but do *not* "burp" bowl. Put in a draft-free place. When seal pops up, about 20 to 30 minutes, add the cup of melted margarine, stirring the complete mixture into all the flour to make a soft dough. Reseal and "burp" the lid. When the top pops up again, 15 to 20 minutes, turn out onto a floured cloth. With floured hands, pat down, taking the air out. Shape into desired shapes and let rise again until doubled.
Baking times: Dinner rolls, 400 degrees, about 12 minutes, Cinnamon rolls, 375 degrees, 25 minutes, Loaves, 350 degrees, 40 to 45 minutes.
Yield: 48, 2-1/2 inch dinner rolls
    OR 24 cinnamon rolls
    OR 3, 9 inch loaves (1-1/2 lbs. each).

Grandma's Menus

Grandma's Quilting Party &
Covered Dish Luncheon

Grandma's quilting circle meets at her house for a fun day of quilting and gossiping. Each one brings their favorite covered dish for their noon-day meal.

Note: In the old days, these were called "Quilting Bees", but when Granny & her friends got together, it was always a PARTY!

Hash Brown Casserole, p. 23
Broccoli Salad, p. 64
Hot Vegetable Salad, p. 66
Chicken Salad Sandwiches, p. 69
Tray of Pimiento Cheese Sandwiches, p. 80
"Devilish" Eggs, p. 62   Watergate Salad, p. 73
Angel Dessert Squares, p. 186

FARMHOUSE SOUPS & SALADS

RECITES:
FARMHOUSE SOUPS

FARMHOUSE SALADS

GRANDMA DEE'S CHILI

1 pound ground beef	3/4 teaspoon black pepper
1 medium onion, diced	1 tablespoon chili powder
1 (15 ounce) can tomato sauce	1 teaspoon cumin
1 (15 ounce) can chopped tomatoes	2 teaspoons salt
1 (15 ounce) can kidney beans, with liquid	1 cup water
1 (15 ounce) can pinto beans, with liquid	
1 (4-1/2 ounce) can chopped green chilies	

Brown the ground beef and onion together in large Dutch oven pot. Stir constantly with large cooking spoon, breaking up meat into small pieces. Drain off liquid. Add all the rest of the ingredients. Cook, covered, over medium low heat, simmering for about 2 hours. Stir often to keep from sticking. Makes 6 to 8 servings. Good accompaniments are: shredded sharp cheese, chopped onions, crumbled Fritos, saltine crackers, skillet hoecakes and Tabasco sauce.

NOTE: After browning meat and onions, you can cook this in a crockpot on low for 8 hours.

MOTHER'S CHILI

1-1/2 pounds ground beef
1 large onion, chopped
2 tablespoons vegetable oil
2 tablespoons chili powder
1 (29 ounce) can chopped tomatoes
1 (29 ounce) can tomato sauce
2 (15 ounce) cans tomato sauce
1 teaspoon salt
3 tablespoons prepared mustard

Brown ground beef and onions in oil. Drain and add rest of the ingredients. Simmer, covered, for 1 hour.

CHICKEN VELVET SOUP

6 tablespoons butter
6 tablespoons all-purpose flour
1/2 cup milk
1/2 cup half & half
3 cups chicken broth
1 cup cooked chicken, finely chopped
Salt & black pepper to taste

Melt butter in medium saucepan over medium heat. Blend in flour, stirring about 1/2 minute to cook flour. Add milk, half & half and broth. Cook, stirring constantly, until mixture thickens and comes to a boil. Reduce heat. Stir in chopped chicken. Add salt and pepper to taste. Heat thoroughly and serve immediately with saltine crackers or little Breakfast Tea Muffins (p. 31) Makes about 5 cups.

OYSTER STEW

1/2 cup butter
1/2 cup chopped onions
1 quart fresh Standard oysters, undrained
1 quart whipping cream
1 pint half & half
Milk, as much as desired
Salt & white pepper

Pick through oysters to make sure there are no shell fragments. *Do not wash oysters.* Melt butter in heavy saucepan; sauté onions in butter till soft. Add oysters, with their juice and cook over low heat *just* until they begin to curl. Then add creams and milk. Heat *just* to the boiling point. Do not boil or milk will curdle. Salt & pepper to taste. Serve with Tabasco Sauce and crackers. Makes 8 servings.

Oyster stew, #2

1 pint Standard oysters	1/2 teaspoon salt
3 tablespoons butter	Black pepper to taste
1 cup half & half	Dash of paprika
3 cups milk, scalded	2 tablespoons butter

Cook oysters and 3 tablespoons butter *in* oyster liquid just until edges curl. Add half & half and milk, heating to boiling point. Season to taste. Sprinkle with paprika and add the 2 tablespoons butter. Serve immediately with saltines and hot pepper sauce. Makes 4 servings

Emery's seafood gumbo

1/4 cup butter	1 bay leaf
1/2 cup chopped onion	1/2 teaspoon dried basil
1/3 cup chopped bell pepper	1/4 teaspoon dried thyme
1/2 cup cubed cook ham	1/4 cup dried parsley
1 cup chicken, cooked & diced	Salt & pepper to taste
2 cups raw okra, sliced	1/2 cup bourbon, optional
1 pint (2 cups) V-8© juice	Steamed rice
1 quart chicken broth	
2 (6 ounce) cans tiny shrimp	
1 pound fresh crabmeat *or*	
2 (6 ounce) cans	

In a large Dutch oven, brown onion, bell pepper, ham, chicken and okra in butter. Add tomato juice, chicken broth, shrimp, crabmeat and spices. Bring to a boil and *simmer,* covered, for 20 minutes. Add bourbon and cook 10 minutes more. Serve over steamed rice. Makes 8 servings.

GRANDMA DEE'S VEGETABLE BEEF SOUP

2 pounds stew meat, cut into small pieces
2 (10-3/4 ounce) cans beef broth
1 (32 ounce) can chopped tomatoes
2 bay leaves
2 (16 ounce) packages frozen gumbo vegetable mix
4 large potatoes, peeled, cubed & cooked
Salt & black pepper to taste

Place the meat, broth, tomatoes, bay leaves and gumbo mix in a large Dutch oven. Cook, over medium heat until meat is fork-tender. (or a crock pot for 8 hours) Meantime, cook potatoes, separately to be sure they get tender. Remove bay leaves, add cooked potatoes *and* the water they're cooked in. (This give you more vitamins!) Serve with crackers and Tabasco sauce.
NOTE: if you don't like okra in your soup, use regular frozen soup vegetable mix. Also, if you don't like tomato chunks in your soup, give them a couple of pulses in your food processor before adding them to the meat.

BOUQUET GARNI

1 tablespoon dried parsley
1 teaspoon dried basil
1 teaspoon dried rosemary
1 teaspoon dried

2 bay leaves
6 whole peppercorns
1 clove fresh garlic

Mix together and place about 2 teaspoons in pieces of cheese-cloth, tied with string. Add to soups or beef stews.

Granny Says:

Sometimes I wake up Grouchy,
and sometimes I let him sleep!

CREAMY POTATO SOUP

6 cups frozen shredded hash brown potatoes
1/2 cup carrots, sliced thin
6 slices bacon
1 medium onion, chopped
2 cups milk
2 cups half & half
Salt & pepper to taste
Finely shredded Cheddar cheese

Cook potatoes and carrots until tender. (I usually cook them separately because carrots take a little longer). Drain; cook bacon until crisp, crumble & set aside. Saute onion in bacon fat. Add cooked potatoes, carrots, milk and half & half. Season to taste with salt & pepper. To serve pour into soup bowls, top with cheese and crumbled bacon. Makes 2 quarts

Optional: As a good supper dish, add 2 cups cooked diced chicken. (you could boil 1 large chicken breast for this if you don't have any left-over chicken.) Diced ham would also be nice.

Emery's Grandmother, Mary Linzy. She was known to her friends as "Miss Kitty" and to her family as "Mammy Linzy".

SENATE BEAN SOUP

When we visited Washington DC in 1979 for our 25th wedding anniversary, we had lunch in the Senate Dining Room. This soup recipe was making the rounds in cookbooks everywhere so I was curious to try it. There are several versions, but this one is supposed to be the one they serve in the U. S. Senate Dining Room.

2 pounds dried navy beans
1 teaspoon salt
1-1/2 pounds of smoked ham hocks
1 large onion, finely chopped

2 tablespoons butter
1/4 teaspoon black
    pepper
Salt to taste

Sort beans, wash well and pick over for rocks, removing any beans that float to the top. Soak beans overnight in enough water to cover by several inches. Next day: Drain beans and place in a Dutch oven. Add enough water to make 4 quarts of liquid. Add ham hocks and bring to a boil. Cover and simmer for about 3 hours, or until tender. Sauté onion in butter until transparent and add to beans. Stir in black pepper. Remove ham hocks and pull meat off bone, cutting into small pieces. Return meat to soup. Add salt to taste when ready to serve. Serve with lots of crusty French bread.   Makes 8 servings.

GREAT-AUNT SUSIE'S "DEVILISH" EGGS

6 large eggs
1/3 cup mayonnaise
1/2 teaspoon dry mustard
1/2 teaspoon salt

6 dashes hot pepper sauce
1 tablespoon sweet pickle relish
1/4 teaspoon black pepper
Paprika for garnish

Boil eggs, peel; cut into halves. Scoop out yolks and mash with a fork. Mix yolks with mayonnaise, mustard, salt, pepper sauce, relish & pepper till smooth. Refill whites with yolk mixture, heaping lightly. Sprinkle paprika on top of each.   Makes 12 halves.

SUMMERTIME ICY GAZPACHO
Grandmother's Garden Soup!

4 cups tomato juice, Welch's is prefered
1 (10-3/4 ounce) can beef broth
2 fresh beefsteak tomatoes
1/2 cup unpeeled cucumbers, chopped
1/4 cup green bell pepper, chopped
1/4 cup sweet onion, (like Vidalia), chopped
1/4 cup wine vinegar
2 tablespoons salad oil
1 teaspoon salt
1 teaspoon Worcestershire sauce
6 drops Tabasco sauce

In a large sauce pan, bring tomato juice and beef broth to boiling; Remove from heat and cool. Peel, seed and dice tomatoes. Add to cooled tomato juice/broth along with rest of ingredients. Refrigerate several hours until cold. Serve in chilled bowls. Garnish with a slice of lemon in each bowl.   Makes 8 servings
NOTE: This is also good hot.

OLD FASHIONED COLESLAW

1 small head cabbage, about 6 cups shredded
2 carrots, grated
1-1/4 cups mayonnaise
2 tablespoons cider vinegar
2 tablespoons sugar
Salt & pepper to taste

Combine mayonnaise, vinegar, and sugar. Mix with carrots and cabbage. Taste for salt & black pepper. Makes 4 cups
Note: Some people like to add onion to their coleslaw. If you like, you can add about 1/2 cup grated onion.

SEAFOOD CHOWDER

1 (6 ounce) can crabmeat
1 (6 ounce) can tiny shrimp
1 fish fillet (preferably Cod), cooked & cut into bite-sized pieces
2 cups diced potatoes
1 cup diced celery
1 cup finely diced onions
3/4 cup butter
3/4 cup all-purpose flour
2 cups milk
2 cups half & half
1-1/2 teaspoons salt
Dash black pepper

Pour crabmeat juice and shrimp juice over vegetables in medium saucepan. Add enough water to cover. Simmer, covered, over medium heat till barely tender. In Dutch oven or similarly large pot, melt butter; add flour and whisk till smooth. Stir to cook for several minutes. Add milk and half & half, whisking constantly till thick and smooth. Add *un*-drained vegetables, crabmeat and shrimp. Season to taste. This makes a lot! Good for dinner, plus lunch for 2 or 3 days.

RAH!! RAH!!
MARISSA!!
2000

CALICO BEAN SALAD

Vegetables: Combine:

1 (16 ounce) can green beans

1 (16 ounce) can wax beans

1 (15 ounce) can kidney beans

1 medium bell pepper, sliced

1 medium onion, sliced

Marinade: Combine in a separate bowl:

1/2 cup vegetable oil

1/2 cup cider vinegar

3/4 cup sugar

1/2 teaspoon salt

1/2 teaspoon black pepper

Pour marinade over vegetable mixture, stirring gently. Cover and chill overnight. Makes 8 to 10 servings.

COLD DILL PEA SALAD

This is good as a salad or a side vegetable.

2 (10 ounce) packages frozen green peas

1 cup sour cream

1/2 teaspoon dried dill weed

1 teaspoon chopped fresh chives or 1/2 teaspoon dried

1/2 teaspoon curry powder

Salt & black pepper to taste

Lemon juice to taste

Cook peas 5 minutes and drain. You want them still crunchy. Mix rest of the ingredients together and carefully fold into the peas.   Makes 8 servings.

Granny's Wisdom:
Warm Cookies and Cold Milk
are Good For You!

Hot vegetable salad

Also a good vegetable side dish

SAUCE: Make this the day before this dish is to be served.
1 cup mayonnaise
1 tablespoon Worcestershire sauce
1 tablespoon prepared mustard
3 tablespoons vegetable oil
2 large eggs, hard boiled and chopped
1 small onion, chopped

Mix together and refrigerate. Take out of the refrigerator and heat thoroughly just before serving.

VEGETABLES:
1 (10 ounce) package frozen petite English peas
1 (10 ounce) package frozen petite lima beans
1 (10 ounce) package frozen French-style green beans

Cook frozen vegetables separately according to package directions and *drain.* Combine *1/2* of the *hot sauce* with the *hot vegetables.* Pour in serving dish and spread rest of the sauce over top. Serve immediately.   Makes 8 to 10 servings.

Shrimp and macaroni salad

2-1/2 cups shrimp, cooked
1 cup cooked macaroni
2 hard-boiled eggs, chopped

3/4 cup mayonnaise
1/4 cup celery, chopped
Salt & pepper to taste

Combine all ingredients. Serve on lettuce leaves, garnishing with whole shrimp.

NOTE: 1/2 cup uncooked macaroni = 1 cup cooked.

Stir and Go Salad

1 (3 ounce) package orange gelatin
1 pound container cottage cheese
1 (8-1/4 ounce) can crushed pineapple, *drained*
1 (11 ounce) can mandarin oranges, *drained*
1 (4 ounce) carton (1-3/4 cups) Cool Whip

Empty dry gelatin into a bowl. Stir in cottage cheese and drained crushed pineapple. Carefully stir in orange slices. Fold in Cool Whip and refrigerate until serving time. Serve on lettuce leaf.
Makes 6 to 8 servings.
Variation: Instead of orange gelatin and oranges, you can substitute strawberry gelatin and strawberries or cherry gelatin and cherries.

Frozen Salad
Good for family get-together dinner.

1 (14 ounce) can sweetened condensed milk (not evaporated)
1 (20 ounce) can crushed pineapple, *drained*
2 cups Cool Whip
Juice of 2 lemons (2 tablespoons)
1 (21 ounce) can Cherry Pie Filling

Mix all together and spread evenly in 9 x 13 inch dish and freeze. To serve, cut into squares and top with Cool Whip.
Makes 12 squares.

Granny Says:
"My mind not only wanders, sometimes it leaves completely"

Hellman's® Classic Macaroni Salad

1 (8 ounce) box elbow macaroni,
    cooked and drained
1 cup sliced celery
1 cup chopped green bell pepper
1/4 cup chopped onion
1 cup mayonnaise

1 tablespoon prepared
    mustard
2 tablespoons cider vinegar
1 tablespoon sugar
1 teaspoon salt
1/8 teaspoon black pepper

In a large bowl, combine first 4 ingredients together. Stir the next 6 ingredients together; add to vegetable mixture and mix well. Cover and chill. Makes 5 cups.

Shrimp Salad

2 pounds medium shrimp
4 ounce jar diced pimiento
1 cup mayonnaise
1 cup chopped celery
1/2 teaspoon Worcestershire
    sauce

1/2 cup chopped green onion
1/2 teaspoon prepared
    mustard
Salt & pepper to taste

Mix all together and serve on lettuce leaves. Makes 6 servings
NOTE: To make shrimp salad sandwiches, pulse in food processor.

Egg Salad or Sandwiches

18 hard-boiled eggs, chopped
2 cups mayonnaise
2 cups pickle relish

1 teaspoon salt
1/2 cup pimiento, chopped

Mix all ingredients together for sandwiches.

Tuna Salad

1 (12 ounce) can tuna, packed in water, well drained
4 large eggs, hard-boiled and chopped
1/2 cup finely chopped celery
1 tablespoon sweet pickle relish
1/2 cup mayonnaise
1 tablespoon lemon juice
Salt & black pepper to taste

Mix all together and use for salad plates or sandwiches.

Chicken Salad

3 pounds cooked chicken, cut into chunks
4 cups finely chopped celery
12 large eggs, hard-boiled and chopped
2-1/2 cups mayonnaise
Salt & black pepper taste

Mix all together and use for salad plates or sandwiches.

Fruit Salad

1 cup shredded coconut
2 cups miniature marshmallows
1 (20 ounce) can chunk pineapple, *drained and cut up*
1 (12 ounce) carton sour cream
Maraschino cherries for garnish

Mix first 3 ingredients together and stir in sour cream. Top with cherries. Pretty served in goblets.

KATIE'S LIME JELL-O® SALAD

2 (6 ounce) packages lime Jell-O®
3 cups boiling water
2 cups crushed pineapple
1/4 cup lemon juice
2 cups cottage cheese
3/4 cup mayonnaise

Dissolve the Jell-O in boiling water. Add rest of the ingredients and pour into lightly greased 9 x 13 inch dish and congeal. Cut into squares.   Makes 12 to 16 servings.

FROZEN CHRISTMAS SALAD
I made this a lot in the 1960'S.

2 (3 ounce) packages cream cheese, softened
1 cup mayonnaise
3-1/2 cups canned fruit cocktail, well-drained
1/2 cup Maraschino cherries, drained and quartered
2-1/2 cups miniature marshmallows
1 cup heavy cream, whipped

Blend softened cream cheese with mayonnaise. Add fruit cock-tail, cherries and marshmallows. Fold in whipped cream. Add a few drops of cherry juice for color. Pour salad mixture into 9 x 13 inch dish. Freeze firm, about 6 hours or overnight.   12 servings
NOTE: Wash & save your large frozen juice containers for a handy tool as follows: Spoon and pack the above mixture into these cans and place in freezer. When frozen and ready to serve, cut the other end of the can off, push the frozen salad out and slice into rounds. (looks very pretty on lettuce leaves.)

SIMPLE ASPARAGUS SALAD
Arrange **fresh asparagus spears** on a plate of lettuce. On each spear put a dab of **mayonnaise** and a strip of **pimiento**.

Overnight Layered Salad

1 head iceberg lettuce, broken into pieces
1 cup diced celery
1 diced green bell pepper
1 (16 ounce) package frozen green peas, defrosted & drained
1 purple onion, diced
1-1/2 to 1-3/4 cups mayonnaise
2 tablespoons sugar
1 cup Parmesan cheese
8 slices bacon, fried crisp & crumbled

In a large glass salad bowl, layer the following: 1/2 of the lettuce, 1/2 of the celery, 1/2 of the bell pepper, 1/2 of the peas and 1/2 of the onions. Spread 1/2 of the mayonnaise on top of this. Sprinkle 1/2 of the sugar, Parmesan cheese and bacon pieces over the mayonnaise. *Repeat* with other half of the ingredients. Refrigerate overnight. Makes 8 servings.

Three Weeks Slaw
A favorite in the 1960's

3 pounds of white cabbage, chopped fine
1 green bell pepper, sliced in rings
2 large onions, sliced
2 cups sugar
Let stand while preparing marinade:
MARINADE:
1 cup vegetable oil
1 cup cider vinegar
1-1/2 tablespoons celery seed
1 tablespoon salt

Bring to a boil and pour hot over cabbage mixture, stirring well. Will keep for 3 weeks in refrigerator.

CAESAR SALAD

1 head of Romaine lettuce, washed, dried & torn Into pieces
5 cups croutons
6 cloves of garlic, minced
1 tablespoon Dijon mustard
2 tablespoons fresh lemon juice
Dash Worcestershire sauce
1/2 cup olive oil
1/4 cup fresh grated Parmesan cheese

Crush *1/2* of the croutons and place in a food processor or large mixer bowl. Add garlic, mustard, lemon juice, and Worcestershire sauce. Process (or beat) until blended. Then slowly add oil pulsing until creamy. Pour over lettuce; add Parmesan cheese and toss in remaining croutons. Serve immediately. Makes 6 servings
Optional: You may add 5 anchovy fillets, rinsed

PIG PICKIN' COLESLAW

2 versions, 1 creamy with a sweet & sour taste and 1 with a sharper vinegar taste. The Pig Pickin' one is the latter.
Combine:
3 cups cabbage, shredded
1 small carrot, grated
1/2 bell pepper, chopped

Dressing #1

1/3 cup sweet or sour cream
2 tablespoons sugar

2 tablespoons apple cider
1/2 teaspoon salt

Mix together until smooth in a small saucepan and heat to blend. Fold into cabbage mixture. Cool & serve.

Dressing #2

3/4 cup sugar
1/4 cup cider vinegar

1/2 teaspoon salt
2 tablespoons water

Mix same as above.

WATERGATE SALAD

A 1970's recipe that became a classic.

1 (5.1 ounce) package Jell-O® Pistachio Pudding & Pie Filling
1 (20 ounce) can crushed pineapple, *with juice*
1 cup miniature marshmallows
1/2 cup pecans, chopped
1-3/4 cups Cool Whip

Stir the pudding mix, pineapple with juice, marshmallows and nuts together in a large bowl till blended. Gently fold in Cool Whip. Refrigerate for one hour or until ready to serve. Makes 8 servings.

WALDORF SALAD

A popular 1950's Christmas salad

Combine:
2 cups diced apples, with peeling
1 tablespoon lemon juice
1 cup diced celery
1 cup dark raisins
1/2 cup coarsely chopped nuts, pecans or walnuts
1/2 cup mayonnaise

Sprinkle apples with lemon juice. Mix all together and serve in a pretty bowl or on a bed of lettuce. Makes 6 servings.

FIVE CUP SALAD

1 cup Mandarin oranges
1 cup miniature marshmallows
1 cup crushed pineapple, drained

1 cup flaked coconut
1 cup sour cream

Combine all ingredients and mix well.

COUNTRY POTATO SALAD

8 large potatoes, cut into small cubes and cooked till tender
6 large eggs, hard-boiled and chopped
1/2 cup sweet pickle relish
Mayonnaise, enough to combine but not soupy
3 tablespoons prepared mustard

Cook potatoes well done, almost to the mashed potato stage.
Mix all ingredients together, stirring well with a big spoon, almost
beating, so that the potatoes loose their shape. Serve warm or
cold. Makes 8 servings.

RED POTATO SALAD

1 pound red "new" potatoes, scrubbed clean
3 large eggs, hard-boiled
5 slices bacon
1 medium onion, finely chopped
1 stalk celery, finely chopped
1 cup mayonnaise
Salt & black pepper to taste

Cook whole potatoes in salted water, fork-tender but still firm.
Cook eggs, cool, peel and chop. Fry bacon and crumble. In a large
serving bowl, combine potatoes, eggs, onion celery, and bacon. Stir
in mayonnaise. Salt & pepper to taste. Chill 1 hour before serving.
Makes 6 servings.   Double for 12 servings.

Granny's Tip:

To jazz up her coleslaw, sometimes Granny
adds a can of tiny shrimp,
drained & rinsed.

German Potato Salad

8 potatoes
8 slices bacon
2 tablespoons all-purpose flour
1/4 cup sugar
2/3 cup water
1/2 cup white wine vinegar
1 cup chopped green onions
Salt & black pepper to taste

Place whole potatoes in big pot of boiling water. Cook until fork tender but still firm. Cool and cut into small cubes. Fry bacon until crisp, reserving grease in skillet. Drain on paper towels and crumble. Add flour, sugar, water and vinegar to grease in skillet and cook, stirring constantly till thick. Add crumbled bacon, potatoes and green onions to skillet. Stir to mix all together and till everything is well heated. Salt & pepper to taste. Serve warm. Makes 8 servings.

Chef 's Salad

1 head iceberg lettuce
1/2 pound baked ham
1/2 pound roast turkey
1/4 pound Cheddar cheese
4 large hard-boiled eggs
1 large fresh tomato

Tear the lettuce into large pieces. Cut ham, turkey, cheese into strips (called julienne cut). Cut eggs into 4 wedges; cut tomato into 4 wedges. Divide lettuce between 4 salad plates. Arrange strips of meat and cheese in a circle with eggs in between. Place a tomato wedge in the center. Serve with Thousand Island dressing. Makes 4 attractive luncheon plates.

Broccoli Salad

This combination of ingredients sound strange, but I had it at a Christmas luncheon and it really is good.

1 bunch of broccoli, cut into bite-size pieces
4 spring onions, sliced into rounds
1/2 cup dark raisins
8 to 10 slices bacon, cooked till crisp and crumbled
1 cup chopped pecans, (optional)

Mix everything together and set aside. Make the dressing:

DRESSING:
1 cup mayonnaise
1/2 cup sugar
2 teaspoons cider vinegar

Mix together and chill at least 1 hour before adding to broccoli mixture. When ready to serve, add to salad and toss to mix
Variation: Add 1/2 cup cheddar cheese, shredded.

Marinated Vegetable Salad

MARINADE:
Combine in a small saucepan and bring to a boil:
1 cup sugar
1/2 cup vegetable oil
3/4 cup cider vinegar
While still hot, pour over these vegetables:

17 ounce can LeSuer English peas   1 cup sliced carrots
16 ounce can French-style beans   1 cup chopped onion
16 ounce can shoe peg corn   1 cup chopped bell
4 ounce jar chopped pimiento   pepper

Marinate in refrigerator overnight. Will keep for several weeks.

ORANGE CONGEALED SALAD

2 (3 ounce) packages orange gelatin
1-3/4 cups hot water
1 (6 ounce) can frozen orange juice, undiluted
2 (11 ounce) cans Mandarin oranges, drained
1 (20 ounce) can crushed pineapple, undrained

Dissolve gelatin in hot water. Stir in undiluted orange juice and cool. Stir in Mandarin oranges and pineapple. Pour into a lightly greased 9 x 13 inch dish and chill until congealed.
TOPPING:
1 (3.4 ounce) package instant lemon pudding & pie filling
2 cups Cool Whip
Prepare the pudding mix according to directions on package. Carefully fold in Cool Whip and spread on top of congealed salad. Chill.   Makes 8 to 10 servings
Optional: you can sprinkle top with 1 cup chopped pecans.

MANDARIN SHERBET SALAD

1 (6 ounce) package orange gelatin
1 cup boiling water
1 pint orange sherbet, softened
1 (11 ounce) can Mandarin oranges, drained
1 (8-1/4 ounce) can crushed pineapple, drained
1 cup miniature marshmallows
1/2 pint whipping cream, whipped

Dissolve the orange gelatin in boiling water. Stir in softened sherbet, stirring until melted. Chill till *partially set.* Fold in orange sections, pineapple and marshmallows. Fold in whipped cream last. Pour in a lightly greased 6 cup mold and chill until firm. Makes 8 servings.
NOTE: You can substitute an 8 ounce carton of Cool Whip for the whipping cream.

Coca-Cola Salad

1 (16 ounce) can pitted dark red sweet cherries, reserve juice
1 (20 ounce) can crushed pineapple, reserve juice
1 (3 ounce) package black cherry-flavored gelatin
1 (3 ounce) package raspberry-flavored gelatin
1 (12 ounce) bottle Coca Cola, chilled
1 cup finely chopped celery
1 cup chopped pecans
2 (3 ounce) packages cream cheese, softened

Drain juice from cherries and pineapple and if not 2 cups of liquid, add enough water to make 2 cups. Heat to boiling and dissolve gelatins. stirring to dissolve. Add Cola. Let congeal *slightly*. Add drained cherries, pineapple, celery and pecans. Beat softened cream cheese till smooth and fluffy and fold into fruit mixture. Pour into a lightly greased 9 x 13 inch dish and congeal till firm. Cut in squares to serve. Makes 15 servings.

Cucumber-Lime Congealedsalad

1 (3 ounce) package lime gelatin
3/4 cup water
3/4 cup cucumber
2 tablespoons onion, grated
1 cup cottage cheese
1 cup mayonnaise
1/3 cup slivered almonds, toasted (op.)

Dissolve gelatin in hot water. Chill till *partially* set. Shred cucumber but do not peel. Strain cucumber and onion together; mix with remainder of ingredients. Fold into chilled gelatin. Pour into lightly greased mold. Chill till firm. Makes 8 to 10 servings.

Tubs O' Shrimp Great for lunch.

Cut the tops off whole fresh tomatoes, scoop out the pulp and fill with peeled, de-veined & cooked shrimp. Replace tops & serve.

BLUEBERRY CONGEALED SALAD

1 (8-1/4 ounce) can crushed pineapple, reserve juice
2 (3 ounce) packages blackberry gelatin
1 (16 ounce) can blueberries, (not pie filling) reserve juice

To the reserved pineapple juice add enough water to make 3 cups.
Put in a saucepan and bring to a boil. Add gelatin and stir well to
dissolve. Chill until *partially* congealed. Add drained blueberries
and drained pineapple. Pour into a lightly greased 9 x 13 dish and
chill until congealed. After it congeals, add the topping below.
Makes 15 squares.

TOPPING:
1 (8 ounce) package cream cheese
1/2 cup sugar
1 (8 ounce) carton sour cream
1 teaspoon vanilla
1/2 cup chopped pecans

Cream together the cream cheese, sugar and sour cream. Stir in
the vanilla. Fold in nuts. Spread evenly over congealed salad.

CREAMY PINEAPPLE-LIME CONGEALED SALAD

1 (3 ounce) package lime gelatin
3/4 cup boiling water
1 (5 ounce) can evaporated milk
1 (8 ounce) can crushed pineapple, with juice
1 tablespoon lemon juice

1 cup cottage cheese
1/2 cup chopped celery
1/2 cup mayonnaise
1/2 cup chopped nuts (op.)

Dissolve gelatin in boiling water. Cool slightly; stir in milk. Chill until *partially set*. Stir in remaining ingredients. Pour into lightly
greased 8 inch square dish. Chill till firm.   Makes 8 servings.

7-UP SALAD

1 (3 ounce) package lime gelatin
1 cup boiling water
1 teaspoon sugar
1 (8 ounce) package cream cheese,
            softened
1 (8-1/4 ounce) can crushed pineapple, drained
1 (7 ounce) bottle 7-UP

1 teaspoon vanilla
1/2 cup chopped
            pecans

Dissolve gelatin in water and stir in sugar. Add cream cheese and beat together to blend. Stir in remaining ingredients and pour into greased 8 or 9 inch square dish. Refrigerate till firm. Makes 6 squares.

PIMIENTO CHEESE FOR SANDWICHES

16 ounces sharp Cheddar cheese, grated
1 (7 ounce) jar diced pimientos, drained
1/8 teaspoon ground red pepper

1/2 teaspoon salt
1/2 cup mayonnaise

Combine all ingredients together, beating well with a spoon until well mixed. Store in refrigerator until ready to use. Makes about 10 sandwiches. Also great for finger sandwiches, for a luncheon or party. Cut the crusts off and cut each sandwich into 3 fingers". Grandma always took these to picnics.

PIMIENTO CHEESE WITH A "BITE"

1-1/4 pounds sharp Cheddar cheese, grated
2 (4 ounce) jars diced pimientos, drained
3 tablespoons mayonnaise
1 (8 ounce) jar Pace picante sauce, hot, medium _or_ mild

Mix everything together. How "hot" is your choice!

RIB-STICKING MAIN DISHES

Dianne & Mom
1934

RECIPES:

NORTH CAROLINA "PIG PICKIN"

A "big deal" in NC! "In it's purest
form a true celebratory event at
which one or more dressed pigs
are slow roasted over coals and
basted with a sauce of cider vinegar and crushed hot peppers. The
succulent meat is picked or
chopped and eaten with great
"gusto"!
(quote from the NC Pork
Producers Association)
A "Pig "Pickin' " menu is on p. 47

MOM'S ROAST BEEF
Makes the BEST gravy!

2 to 3 pound beef roast
1 (10-3/4 ounce) can cream of mushroom soup
1 envelope onion soup mix
1 cup water

Preheat oven to 350 degrees. Sear roast in deep pan in 2 table-spoons oil mixed with 2 tablespoons butter. Mix the soup, dry soup mix and water together and pour over meat, lifting to get some underneath. Cover and bake in preheated oven exactly 2 hours. This size roast will be fork-tender in 2 hours. If roast is larger increase baking time 30 minutes per pound more.

MEATLOAF WITH VEGETABLES
Campbell Soup published this recipe in the 1950's. Moist & good.

2 pounds ground beef
1 tablespoon Worcestershire sauce
1 (10-3/4 ounce) can Campbell's vegetable soup
1 large egg, beaten
1/2 cup soft bread crumbs
1 medium onion, chopped
1 tablespoon prepared mustard
1 teaspoon salt
1/4 teaspoon black pepper

Preheat oven to 350 degrees. Mix all ingredients together and shape into a 9 inch loaf pan. Bake in preheated oven for 1 hour. Makes 10 servings.

MOM'S MEATLOAF

1 pound ground beef
1 pound ground pork
1/2 cup finely chopped onion
1 tablespoon Worcestershire sauce
1 tablespoon milk
1 teaspoon dry mustard
1/2 cup fresh bread crumb

1 teaspoon salt
1/2 teaspoon pepper
2 tablespoons parsley
1/4 teaspoon nutmeg
1 large egg, beaten
1/2 cup medium salsa

Preheat oven to 350 degrees. Mix everything together except the salsa. Mix well. Mold into a 9 inch loaf pan. Pour salsa evenly on top. Bake in preheated oven for 1 hour.   Makes 6 to 8 servings.

COUNTRY-STYLE BEEF STEW

2 pounds lean stew meat
Garlic salt
Black pepper
2 tablespoons oil
1 large onion, chopped
1 (16 ounce) can Italian seasoned stewed tomatoes
3 carrots, cut into chunks
2 (10-3/4 ounce) cans beef broth
2 large potatoes, cut into large cubes

Sprinkle meat with garlic salt and black pepper. Cook meat in oil, stirring constantly till it's brown. Add onion, tomatoes, carrots, and beef broth and cook till meat is tender, about 1 hour. In a separate saucepan cook potatoes till tender but still firm. Taste for seasoning but remember beef broth has salt. If you want a thicker gravy, dilute about 1 tablespoon of cornstarch in a small amount of water and add to the pot.   Makes 8 servings.

Mother's "Puffy" Dumplings for Stew

1 cup all-purpose flour	1 large egg
1/2 teaspoon baking powder	1/3 cup milk
1/2 teaspoon salt	2 tablespoons oil

Sift flour, baking powder and salt together. Combine egg, milk and oil, beating with a fork to mix. Add to dry ingredients to make a soft dough. Drop by tablespoonfuls into hot stew Do this when the stew meat is fork-tender. You should have plenty of liquid. Cover and cook for 15 minutes WITHOUT peeking!

Mother's Spaghetti Sauce

My mother *never* shared her recipes, except with me. So all of the recipes in this book called "Mother's" are hers!

2 tablespoons oil	Salt & black pepper
1 medium bell pepper, chopped	1/2 teaspoon oregano
1 medium onion, chopped	
1 clove garlic	
1 pound hamburger	
1 (6 ounce) can tomato sauce, plus 2 cans water	
1 (6 ounce) can tomato paste, plus 2 cans water	
1 (4 ounce) can mushroom pieces, plus 2 cans water	

In a large skillet or Dutch oven sauté the bell pepper, onion, and garlic in the oil. Add meat and brown, stirring to crumble. Add salt, pepper and oregano. Add tomato sauce, paste, mushrooms and cans of water called for. Cover and simmer at least 2 hours. Cook a 16 ounce package of spaghetti as directed on the package. Rinse under hot water in a colander and serve with the above sauce and grated Parmesan cheese.
Makes 8 servings.

MEATBALLS FOR SPAGHETTI

If you prefer meatballs in you sauce instead of crumbled meat.

1 pound ground beef	1/4 cup finely chopped onions
1 pound ground pork	1 teaspoon salt
3/4 cup dry bread crumbs	1/4 teaspoon black pepper
1/4 cup milk	1/4 teaspoon nutmeg
1 large egg	

Mix everything together and shape into about 2 inch balls. Replace the hamburger meat with these meatballs and simmer in Mother's sauce for 2 hours.

Option: For an appetizer you can shape these in 1 inch balls. Place on an ungreased 10x15 jelly roll pan and bake uncovered at 350 degrees for 20 minutes. Then place in a crock-pot filled with sweet & sour sauce (below) or your favorite bottled barbeque sauce. Great for a party, covered dish or family gathering.

SWEET & SOUR SAUCE

1-1/2 cups apple juice	2 tablespoons soy sauce
1/3 cup cider vinegar	1/4 teaspoon salt
1/4 cup sugar	2 tablespoons cornstarch
1/4 cup catsup	1/4 cup more apple juice

Combine everything except the cornstarch and 1/4 cup apple juice in a medium saucepan. Stir the cornstarch into the 1/4 cup apple juice and add to sauce. Simmer to thicken.

Granny says:

No matter how hard you try, you can't baptize cats!

MOTHER'S SWISS STEAK

This was one of Mother's specialties and became my "company" dinner specialty when I married. It still gets raves.

1-1/2 to 2 pounds round steak, cut 2 inches thick
4 tablespoons all-purpose flour
1 teaspoon salt
1/8 teaspoon black pepper
3 tablespoons vegetable oil
1 (14.5 ounce) can stewed tomatoes
1/2 cup chopped celery
1/2 cup chopped onions
1/2 cup grated carrots
2 tablespoons chopped parsley
1/2 teaspoon Worcestershire sauce
1 (4 ounce) can mushroom stems & pieces, undrained
1 cup water

Pat steak with damp paper towels and cut into serving pieces. Combine flour, salt & pepper; pound into steak pieces; reserving flour. Heat oil in large skillet. Brown meat. Remove and stir reserved flour into drippings. Add steak back to skillet and add rest of the ingredients. Bring to a boil. Reduce heat and simmer about 2 hours or until steak is tender, stirring occasionally. Makes about 6 servings.

NOTE: This can be done in a 350 degree oven for the same amount of time. I prefer the oven method as anything with cooked tomatoes tend to stick to the pan and burn.

Serving suggestions: Mashed potatoes, green vegetable, tossed salad and hot buttered rolls.

Granny Says:

Don't sneeze while someone is cutting your hair!

DEE PEDDICORD'S LASAGNA

My sister-in-law's recipe.... one of the best cooks ever!

SAUCE:

1 pound ground beef
2 tablespoons vegetable oil
2-1/2 cups canned tomatoes
1 (8 ounce) can tomato sauce

2 cloves garlic
1-1/2 teaspoons salt
1/2 teaspoon black pepper
1/4 teaspoon oregano

Brown the ground beef in the oil in a large skillet. Add rest of the ingredients and stir together well. Cover and simmer for 30 minutes.

THEN: Cook **1/2 pound lasagna noodles** in salted water, cooking slowly so the noodles will not tear . When tender, drain and rinse under cold water.

Preheat oven to 375 degrees. In a buttered 9 x 13 inch baking dish, put the following in **_alternate layers:_**

Noodles
1 pound cottage cheese
1/2 pound mozzarella cheese
The above meat sauce

Repeat. The top layer should be meat sauce with parmesan cheese sprinkled over it. Bake at 375 degrees for 25 minutes.   Makes 8 servings.

Grandpa Emery with his Dad, who lived to be 100½. This picture was taken Dec. 1998, when he was 99 years old!

Bar-b-q Sauce

1 cup catsup
1 cup strong coffee
1/4 cup butter
1/2 cup Worcestershire sauce

1 tablespoon sugar
1/2 teaspoon salt
1 teaspoon black pepper

In a medium saucepan, combine all of the above. Bring to a boil, stirring with a whisk. Reduce heat and simmer, uncovered, for 30 minutes, stirring frequently. Makes 2 cups.

North Carolina Bar-b-q Sauce

Eastern-style (vinegar based)
North Carolinians are *serious* about their barbecue sauce, each part of the state *swearing* theirs is the best! We've included both, you be the judge!

2 cups cider vinegar
1 tablespoon Tabasco sauce
1 tablespoon chili powder
3 tablespoons black pepper
3/4 teaspoon dry mustard
1 tablespoon Worcestershire sauce

3 tablespoons salt
2 tablespoons paprika
1 (14 ounce) bottle catsup

Simmer all of the above on low heat for 45 minutes to blend flavors and to thicken. For a thinner sauce, add 1/2 cup water. This recipe makes 1 quart and can be multiplied many times to make as much as you wish. Keeps very well in the fridge.

NOTE: In North Carolina, they always serve hush puppies with their barbecue. The menu usually consists of barbecue, French fries, Brunswick stew, coleslaw and hush puppies.

NOTE: For a family meal, cook a 4 to 5 pound Boston butt in a crock-pot for about 10 hours.

NORTH CAROLINA BAR-B-Q SAUCE

Western-style (catsup based)

1 cup catsup
1 cup light brown sugar
1/2 cup lemon juice
1/4 cup butter
1 teaspoon Worcestershire sauce

1/4 cup onion, minced
1 teaspoon Tabasco sauce
  or Texas Pete

Place all ingredients in a heavy sauce pan and bring to a boil.
Reduce heat and simmer for 30 minutes. Makes 3 cups of sauce.

LEXINGTON, NORTH CAROLINA– STYLE COLESLAW

North Carolinians *also* put coleslaw on their Bar-B-Q sandwiches;
something this South Georgia gal is still not used to!
Try it, you might like it. Lexington, North Carolina is *famous* for
it's Bar-B-Q. There must be umpteen dozen Bar-B-Q restaurants
there!

This is a tangy, vinegar-based slaw.

1/2 cup sugar
1/2 cup catsup
1/2 cup white vinegar
1/4 cup vegetable oil
1/4 teaspoon salt
1/4 teaspoon garlic powder

1/2 of a large head of cabbage,
           shredded
1 green bell pepper, coarsely
           chopped

Combine sugar, catsup, vinegar, oil, salt and garlic powder in a
large saucepan. Heat thoroughly, over medium heat, until everything is melted, stirring constantly with a whisk. Pour hot mixture
over cabbage and bell pepper and stir well. Refrigerate at least 2
hours.
*NOTE: A 16 ounce bag of coleslaw mix may be substituted for the
cabbage and bell pepper.*

Chicken and Dumplings

Wash a **3 pound fryer** well. Fill a large pot 2/3 full of water and add a little salt. Place fryer and **1 stick margarine or butter** in pot and bring water to a boil. Cook chicken on medium low heat until chicken is tender. Be sure chicken is really done, almost falling off the bone. Add more water along, if needed. Remove chicken from pot and set aside to cool so you can handle. When cool, tear off in bite-sized chunks. discarding skin and bones.

Boil **6 large eggs**, slice and set aside. While chicken is cooking, make dumplings:

DUMPLINGS:
1 cup all-purpose flour   **1 egg, slightly beaten**
1/4 teaspoon salt   **1/4 cup hot chicken broth**

Mix flour and salt together; add broth and stir, mixing well. Knead slightly and roll out very thin on a floured cloth. Cut into strips, then squares with a pizza cutter. (easier than a knife) Bring the chicken broth to a boil again and drop dumplings into boiling broth. Drop one piece at a time so they will stay separated. Cook at medium heat until fork tender. Then add the chicken pieces and sliced eggs to pot with dumplings. Cover and let sit until ready to serve. The broth will thicken as it sits, because the dumplings absorb the liquid. Makes 6 servings. Good served with hot buttered skillet cornbread (p. 51) or cornbread muffins (p. 50)

Granny's Tip:

Keep plenty of soups in your pantry, especially the "cream of" variety.
Diluted with water or milk, they can make many quick casseroles. With beef or chicken broth, diluted, you can make great gravies!

Sunday Dinner Chicken

2-1/2 to 3 pound fryer, cut into serving pieces
Vegetable oil (just enough to brown chicken pieces)
2 (10-3/4 ounce) cans chicken broth
1 clove garlic, minced
1/4 teaspoon rosemary   3 slices of lemon
3 sliced carrots   2 tablespoons parsley

Season, flour and brown chicken in oil in a Dutch oven. Remove chicken and drain off all but 2 tablespoons drippings. Add chicken broth , minced garlic and rosemary. Replace chicken and add carrots, lemon slices and parsley. Cover and simmer for 30 minutes. Makes 6 servings.   Add mashed potatoes and a green vegetable.

Chicken A La King

A popular 1950's supper dish and also on Diner menus!

5 cups leftover roasted chicken or turkey
1/3 cup butter
1/2 pound sliced mushrooms
1/2 cup diced green bell pepper
2 (10-3/4 ounce) cans cream of chicken soup, undiluted
2 cups half and half
1 (10-3/4 ounce) can frozen green peas, thawed and uncooked
1/2 cup diced pimiento (can be canned)
Salt & black pepper to taste
Toast cups*** (see below)

In a 4 quart pan, melt the butter; add mushrooms and peppers and cook until tender. Stir in soup and half & half. Add chicken, peas and pimento. Salt & pepper taste. Heat thoroughly and serve in toast cups, on toasted bread or split biscuits. Makes 6 servings
*** Cut crusts off bread, brush with melted butter. Press into a muffin pan and toast in 350 degree oven for 15 to 20 minutes.

BUTTERMILK FRIED CHICKEN

Grandpa Emery's "scientific" way to cook the best Southern fried chicken you'll ever eat!

2-1/2 to 3 pound chicken fryer
Salt & black pepper
Light type cooking oil
Buttermilk
All-purpose flour

Cut up, wash and pat chicken dry with paper towels. Salt and pepper and place in a baking pan. Cover with cold water and let stand for 30 minutes. (this gives the salt time to penetrate into the chicken) Fill a Dutch oven with light cooking oil, deep enough to cover chicken well, at least 4 inches. Preheat oven to 350 degrees. (a candy thermometer is good for this) Remove chicken from water, dip briefly in buttermilk, then roll in flour, coating well. Place in hot oil, about 6 pieces at a time, and fry for about 10 minutes or until pieces are golden brown and rise to the top. When the chicken floats, it is done. Turn at least once during the cooking process. Remove chicken from pot and place in colander to drain. (placing on paper towels makes it soft instead of crispy. Serve hot with Fig Preserves (p. 24)

Grandpa Emery's broadcast career began in 1946. This picture was taken in 1953.

KING RANCH CASSEROLE

A popular Texas recipe. Another good way to use left-over chicken.

2 cups cooked diced chicken
1/2 (14.5 ounce) can tomatoes with green chilies
1 (14.5 ounce) can cream of chicken soup, undiluted
1 (14.5 ounce) can cream of mushroom soup, undiluted
1/2 (14.5 ounce) can chicken broth
1 package flour tortillas, cut into small pieces
1 large onion, chopped
8 ounces sharp Cheddar cheese, grated

Preheat oven to 350 degrees. In a greased 9 x13 inch baking dish, layer 1/2 each: chicken, tomatoes, soups, tortillas and onions. Repeat layers. Top with grated cheese. Bake in preheated oven for 1 hour. Makes 8 servings.

Grandma Dee,
Dianne C. Evans
1951

SOUTHERN BAKED CHICKEN & CORNBREAD DRESSING
A North Georgia 1956 recipe

3-1/2 to 4 pound chicken, cooked, de-boned and set aside

2 cups crumbled cornbread (cornbread, p. 51)
1-1/2 cups dry bread crumbs
3 large eggs, slightly beaten
1/2 cup butter, melted
1/2 cup finely diced onion
2 tablespoons chopped celery
3-1/2 to 4 cups chicken broth
1 teaspoon salt
1/8 teaspoon black pepper
1-1/2 teaspoon sage or poultry seasoning

Preheat oven to 450 degrees. Combine all ingredients except chicken, mixing well. Pour 1/2 of the dressing into a greased 9 x 13 inch baking dish. Cut chicken into large pieces and place on top of dressing. Add other 1/2 of the dressing to dish. Bake in preheated oven for 30 minutes.   Makes about 8 servings.

EASY APRICOT CHICKEN

6 chicken breasts
1 (10 ounce) jar apricot
    preserves

1 packet Lipton soup mix
1 (12 ounce) bottle Russian
    salad dressing

Preheat oven to 350 degrees. Mix preserves, dry soup mix and salad dressing together and combine with chicken. Place in a 9 x 13 inch baking dish and bake in preheated oven for 1 hour. Makes 4 to 6 servings.
Serve with steamed rice and green vegetable or green salad.

CHICKEN PILAU

Churches *always* had chicken pilau suppers as a money-making project. (pronounced per'loo or per'low)

3-1/2 pound fryer
2 celery ribs, cut in big pieces
2 carrots, cut in big pieces
1 medium onion, coarsely chopped
1 teaspoon salt
1/2 teaspoon garlic salt
1/2 teaspoon black pepper
Water to cover chicken
1 cup long-grain rice, uncooked (we prefer Uncle Ben's)
6 hard-cooked eggs, chopped

In a large Dutch oven combine chicken, celery, carrots, onion, salts, and black pepper. Cover with water. Bring to a boil; then reduce heat to medium low and simmer till chicken is tender. (about 1 hour) Remove chicken and cool enough to remove meat from bone, discarding skin and bones. Cut chicken into bite-sized pieces. Remove all but about 2 cups of the broth. Cook rice in broth until desired doneness. Return chicken pieces to pot along with chopped eggs. Stir gently to combine.
Makes about 6 servings or 4 hungry appetites.
Serve with cornbread muffins or hoecake

TUNA-MACARONI CASSEROLE

2 cups elbow macaroni, cooked
1 (10-3/4 ounce) can cream of mushroom soup
1 (12 ounce) can evaporated milk
1 cup shredded sharp Cheddar Cheese
1 cup croutons, crushed

Preheat oven to 350 degrees. Combine macaroni, soup & milk. Pour in greased 9 x 13 inch casserole. Top with cheese & croutons. Bake in preheated oven for 20 to 30 minutes till bubbly & brown.

CHICKEN PIE

No Grandma cookbook would be complete with old-fashioned Chicken Pie. There are many, many variations of this favorite dish. Some add mixed vegetables, some only English peas. Grandma thought it was good enough to stand on it's own without a lot of extra "stuff". We've added English peas. You could add some pearl onions, sliced mushrooms and/or some small potato cubes or some mixed frozen vegetables.

4 cups cooked chicken, cut into bite-sized pieces
6 tablespoons butter
6 tablespoons all-purpose flour
1 cup milk
2 cups chicken broth
Salt & black pepper to taste
1 cup canned English peas
1 Pillsbury All-Ready Pie Crust (1/2 of 15 ounce box)

Preheat oven to 425 degrees. Melt butter in medium saucepan. Add the flour and cook, stirring for about 1 minute. Slowly add milk and chicken broth, making a white sauce. Add salt & black pepper to taste. Cook until thickened, about 5 minutes.
Add peas to chicken and place in bottom of a 9 x 13 inch baking dish. Cover with sauce. Unfold pie crust and roll to fit top of baking dish. Cover filling completely. Cut steam vents in top. Rubbing a little milk on top of crust makes a pretty golden baked crust. Bake in preheated oven for 25 to 30 minutes. Makes 6 servings

Variation: Country-style— make 1 recipe of biscuit dough (p. 27) Roll out biscuit dough 1/2 inch thick. Cut out biscuits and place on top of filling. Bake at 450 degrees for 15 minutes.

CHICKEN & RICE CASSEROLE

2-1/2 pound chicken fryer, cut up
1 cup raw long grain rice (not instant; we use Uncle Ben's)
1 (10-3/4 ounce) can cream of celery soup
1 (10-3/4 ounce) can cream of chicken soup
1-1/2 soup cans water
1 envelope dry onion soup mix

Preheat oven to 350 degrees. Mix rice, soups and 1-1/2 soup cans of water together and pour into a greased 9 x 13 inch baking dish. Lay raw chicken pieces on top of rice mixture. Sprinkle dry onion soup mix evenly over top. Cover tightly with foil and bake in preheated oven for 1 hour and 45 minutes. It takes this long to get the rice done.   Serves 6 to 8.

TUNA CASSEROLE

I saved many a food budget with this...Grandpa sill asks for it!

Mashed potatoes (can be left-over)
1 (12 ounce) can chunk, water-packed tuna, well-drained
1 (16 ounce) can English peas
1 (10-3/4 ounce) can cream of mushroom soup, undiluted

Preheat oven to 350 degrees. In a lightly greased 9 inch loaf pan, layer: 1/2 of the mashed potatoes, 1/2 of the can of tuna, 1/2 English peas, 1/2 can mushroom soup. Repeat layers. Cover and put into preheated oven and bake for 30 minutes until everything is hot and bubbly. Serves 6.
NOTE: You can cook a package of flat noodles and substitute that for the mashed potatoes.

CHICKEN PARMIGIANA

Parmigiana (par' me zhan') means covered with or made of Parmesan cheese.

6 boneless & skinless chicken breasts
3 large eggs, slightly beaten
1 teaspoon salt
1/8 teaspoon black pepper
1 cup dry bread crumbs
1 (15 ounce) container DiGiorno Marinara Sauce (found in the
   dairy case)
1 (8 ounce) package (8 deli-thin slices) Kraft Mozzarella slices
   (found in the dairy case), cut each slice into triangles
1/2 cup grated parmesan cheese
8 ounce package fettuccini or spaghetti noodles

Preheat oven to 350 degrees. Combine eggs, salt & pepper. Dip each chicken breast in egg mixture and roll in bread crumbs. Brown in hot oil in skillet and drain. Place breasts in lightly greased 9 x 13 inch baking dish. Pour Marinara sauce over chicken and sprinkle with parmesan cheese. Cover and bake in preheated oven for 30 minutes. *Uncover* and arrange mozzarella cheese triangles on top. Bake, uncovered, for 10 more minutes. *Meanwhile* cook fettuccini noodles in water with a little salt added. Drain, toss with butter and serve with chicken. Makes 6 servings.

SCHOOL
DAYS

DAVID THOMAS, 1999

NATALIE, 2001

CHICKEN & BROCCOLI CASSEROLE

6 chicken breasts, cooked and cut in large pieces
2 (10 ounce) packages frozen broccoli spears
1/2 cup sharp Cheddar cheese, shredded
1 cup buttered soft bread crumbs

Preheat oven to 350 degrees. Cook broccoli according to package directions. Arrange in buttered 9 x 13 inch baking dish. Top with cooked chicken pieces. Pour sauce (below) over chicken/broccoli. Combine cheese and bread crumbs and sprinkle evenly over top. Bake in preheated oven for 25 to 30 minutes. This dish can be put together ahead of time and cooked just be serving.
Serves 6.

SAUCE;
2 (10-3/4 ounce) cans cream of chicken soup
1 (4 ounce) can mushroom pieces
1 cup mayonnaise
1/2 teaspoon curry powder

Combine all above ingredients together.

Grandpa Emery
catches "the big one"
1996

Big bertha

Mrs. Fred Hamilton gave me this recipe to cook for her guests when I cooked for her at Horseshoe Plantation. It was a great accompaniment for grilled quail. As a main dish, you could add 2 whole cooked chicken breasts, cut into pieces. No, I don't know where the name came from!

2 cups diced green chilies, seeded
2 onions, diced
2 cups canned chopped tomatoes
1 teaspoon sugar
Salt, black pepper and Accent to taste
8 ounces sharp Cheddar cheese, grated
8 ounces Longhorn cheese, gated
1 pint whipping cream
1 package Fritos

Preheat oven to 400 degrees. Sauté onions in a small amount of oil. Mix with peppers, tomatoes, sugar and seasonings. Mix together the two cheeses. Butter a 9 x 13 inch baking dish. Crumble a layer of Fritos in bottom; next a layer of 1/2 of the vegetable mixture; next a layer of 1/2 of the cheeses; next a layer of Fritos, vegetables and cheeses. *Just before baking*, pour cream on top. Bake *uncovered* in preheated oven for 1 hour. Makes 12 servings.

Morgan visits Grandma and Grandpa in Boone, 1999

Stuffed Pork Chops

6 center cut pork chops, 1 inch thick, slit a "pocket" in each
DRESSING:
1 cup soft bread crumbs
1/4 cup chopped celery
1/4 cup chopped onion
1/4 teaspoon salt
1/8 teaspoon paprika
Enough milk to moisten dressing

Preheat oven to 350 degrees. Fill "pockets" with dressing and fasten with toothpicks. Sear in a little oil in a hot skillet; place in 9 x 13 inch baking dish.
Dilute:
1 (10-3/4 ounce) can cream of mushroom soup
with 1/3 cup milk
Pour this soup mixture over pork chops. Cover and bake in pre-heated oven for 1 hour.   Makes 5 servings.

Mom's Oyster Casserole

2 cups crushed saltines   4 hard-cooked eggs, sliced
2 pints fresh oysters, with liquid   Salt & pepper to taste
4 tablespoons butter   Milk

Preheat oven to 350 degrees. In a 1-1/2 quart baking dish, layer: 1/3 of the saltines, 1/2 of the oysters, reserving juice, 1/2 of the sliced eggs, and dot wit 1/2 of the butter. Sprinkle a little salt & pepper. Repeat layers, ending with saltine crackers. Pour oyster juice and enough milk to cover top. Bake *uncovered* in preheated oven for 30 minutes   Makes 6 to 8 servings.

SALMON CROQUETTES

1 (14-3/4 ounce) can pink salmon, undrained
1/2 cup saltine cracker crumbs
1/4 cup plain cornmeal
1 large egg, slightly beaten
1/4 teaspoon each salt & black pepper
Oil for frying

Drain salmon, reserving liquid. Combine cracker crumbs and the reserved salmon liquid. Let stand 5 minutes or until liquid is absorbed by the crackers. Stir in the flaked salmon, cornmeal, egg, salt & pepper. Shape into 6 oval patties. Pour oil to 1/4 inch in heavy skillet and heat to medium heat. Fry patties until brown, turning once. Drain on paper towels. Makes about 6 patties
NOTE: This is a great family dinner with scalloped potatoes or macaroni & cheese and a green vegetable or tossed salad.

SALMON CROQUETTES #2

This is the 1950's recipe. It's really better if you want to go to the trouble of making the simple white sauce (below).

1 (14-3/4 ounce) can pink salmon
1 cup thick white sauce* (see below)
1 tablespoon lemon juice

Saltine crackers,
finely crushed
1 large egg, beaten

Drain salmon, saving liquid. Discard skin. Make white sauce with *recipe below.* Add white sauce and lemon juice to salmon and mix well. Cool. Shape into thick oval patties. Roll in cracker crumbs, dip in egg and roll in crumbs again. Heat about 1/4 inch of oil to medium hot in skillet and fry patties. Makes about 6 patties.

*WHITE SAUCE: Pour reserved salmon juice in 1 cup measuring cup. Add enough milk to fill top of cup. Make sauce with **4 tablespoons butter, 4 tablespoons flour** and **the cup of liquid,** stirring till thickened.

MOTHER'S STUFFED BELL PEPPERS

4 large bell peppers
1/2 medium bell pepper
1 medium onion, chopped
2 tablespoons oil

1 pound ground beef
Salt & pepper to taste
1 (6 ounce) can tomato sauce

Preheat oven to 350 degrees. Parboil peppers for 10 minutes.
Cut a nice sized top off each one. Cook the bell pepper and onion
in 2 tablespoons oil for about 3 minutes until soft but not brown.
Add ground beef, salt & pepper. Stuff the whole bell peppers with
this mixture and pour tomato sauce evenly over each one.
Replace cut-off tops. Put stuffed peppers in a 9x13 inch baking
dish and bake until done, about 1 hour.   Makes 4 servings.

CRABMEAT CASSEROLE

2 cups crabmeat
2 cups finely chopped celery
1 cup mayonnaise
1 cup bread crumbs, toasted
1/2 teaspoon salt

2 tablespoons lemon juice
1 teaspoon grated onion
Crushed potato chips
1/2 cup grated cheese

Preheat oven to 425 degrees. Mix crabmeat, celery, mayonnaise,
bread crumbs, salt, lemon juice and onion together. Place in a
greased 2 quart baking dish. Combine crushed potato chips and
grated cheese and sprinkle on top of casserole. Bake in preheated oven for 15 minutes.   Makes 6 servings.

FAMILY-STYLE VEGETABLES, SIDES & CASSEROLES

RECIPES:

Dianne and her proud Mom & Dad. Wedding Day, 1954

BAKED VIDALIA ONIONS

Vidalia onions, 1 per person (or other medium size sweet onion)
Butter
Salt & pepper
Worcestershire sauce

Preheat oven to 350 degrees. Peel onions and core 3/4 down in center. Sprinkle with salt & pepper. Fill cavity with about 2 tablespoons butter and 1 teaspoon Worcestershire sauce. Wrap each onion separately in a square piece of foil and place on baking sheet. Bake in preheated oven about 45 minutes or until onion is fork-tender. A great side dish for a steak dinner.

CRISPY FRIED VIDALIA ONIONS

3 large Vidalia onions, sliced into 1/4 inch slices
1 quart milk
2 cups all-purpose flour
1/2 teaspoon salt
1/2 teaspoon black pepper
Oil to fry

Slice onions into 1/4 inch slices and separate rings. Place in a large bowl and cover with milk. In a brown paper bag or large plastic bag combine the flour, salt and pepper. Drain onions and shake in the flour mixture (in bag). In a large skillet, heat 1 inch oil to about 375 degrees. Fry onions a few at a time till crisp, about 3 minutes. Drain on paper towels and eat 'em while they're hot!

Ask Granny:

Dear Granny: What is a "Vidalia" onion?
Answer: A Vidalia onion is a sweet onion, developed and grown primarily in Vidalia, GA Check their website, www.vidaliaonions.com.

CREAMY ENGLISH PEAS

2 tablespoons butter
1-1/2 tablespoons all-purpose flour
1/2 cup milk or half & half
1/2 teaspoon salt
1 (17 ounce) can English peas, undrained

Melt butter in medium saucepan. Add flour and stir with whisk for about 1 minute. Stir in milk, stirring until smooth. Add undrained peas and salt. Cook, stirring constantly, till thickened.
Makes about 4 servings.

POTATO PANCAKES

2 medium potatoes, grated
1 tablespoon lemon juice
1/4 cup melted butter
2 tablespoons flour
1/2 cup finely diced onion
1/4 teaspoon baking powder
1 large egg, beaten
1/2 teaspoon salt
1/4 teaspoon black pepper

In a large skillet (or electric skillet) heat to medium with 1 tablespoon oil and 1 tablespoon butter. Add heaping tablespoonfuls of potato mixture to the pan and using the tines of a fork, flatten out each portion to very thin round pancakes, about 2-1/2 inches. Cook 3 to 4 minutes on each side, turning once.
Makes 16 pancakes.
Good accompaniment for meatloaf, steak, fried pork chops or any meal that doesn't have gravy and you need a "starch" vegetable.

PLATT'S BAKED BEANS

Charlotte Platt's husband is one of the best out-door cooks. This is one of his specialties. We changed it just slightly for our own taste.

2-3 slices bacon
1 medium onion, chopped
1 (3# 5 oz.) can Pork & Beans
3/4 cup Hickory Barbeque sauce
5 teaspoons Jalapeno mustard

1 cup light brown sugar
3 tablespoons catsup
5 tablespoons Worcester-
   shire sauce

Preheat oven to 350 degrees. Cut up bacon in small pieces and fry, adding the chopped onion half way through to saute; set aside. Drain beans well and add the 3/4 cup Hickory Barbeque Sauce, mustard, brown sugar, catsup, Worcestershire sauce, bacon and onion, mixing well. Pour into a 9 x 13 baking dish and bake, uncovered, for 1 hour.

NOTE: Mr. Platt's gives optional ingredients of **3/4 cup Hot Pace Picate Sauce and 3/4 cup hot barbeque sauce.** This makes it quite a bit hotter. Our crowd liked it hotter. Try it both ways to see your preference. Doubled, the recipe fills a 5 quart crockpot and makes about 20 to 24 servings, enough for a crowd.

HARVARD BEETS

In the 1940's this was served at every "Banquet"!

2-1/2 cups cooked beets, (15 ounce can)
1/3 cup sugar
2 teaspoons cornstarch

1/4 cup vinegar
1/4 cup beet juice
1 tablespoon butter

In a medium saucepan, mix sugar, cornstarch, vinegar and 1/4 cup beet juice together until smooth. Add butter and cook, over medium heat until thickened, stirring constantly. Add beets and cook just until heated through.   Makes 4 servings.

CORN PUDDING

3 large eggs
2 cups milk
1/2 cup half & half
1 tablespoon sugar
1 teaspoon salt

3 cups whole kernel corn (fresh,
frozen or canned (drained if
using canned)
1/4 cup fresh bread crumbs
2 tablespoons butter

Preheat oven to 350 degrees. Beat eggs till light & fluffy. Add milk, cream, sugar and salt. Stir in corn, bread crumbs and butter. Pour into a greased 1-1/2 quart baking dish. Bake in preheated oven for about 1 hour.   Makes 6 servings.

CORN CASSEROLE WITH CHEESE

1 (14.5 ounce) can creamed corn
1/2 cup butter, melted
2 large eggs, beaten
1/2 cup cornmeal

1/2 teaspoon onion salt
1 cup sour cream
1 cup Cheddar cheese,
shredded

Preheat oven to 350 degrees. Mix all of the above together and pour into a greased 8 inch square baking dish. Bake in preheated oven for about 1 hour. Makes 4 servings.

FRIED CREAMED CORN (SKILLET)

6 ears fresh corn
1/2 to 3/4 stick butter
Salt & pepper to taste

1/2 teaspoon sugar
Milk, about 1/2 to 3/4 cup

With a very sharp knife, cut off just the *tips* of the corn into a bowl. Scrap the cob till you have removed all of the remaining pulp (kernels). Melt butter in a large skillet, add corn and cook over medium-low heat, stirring constantly, about 10 minutes. Add salt, pepper, sugar & milk. Cook about 5 minutes more. Serves 8.

HASH BROWN CASSEROLE

This is the larger recipe.

1 (2 pound) package frozen, shredded hash browns, thawed
1 (10-3/4 ounce) cream of chicken soup
2 cups sour cream
2 cups sharp Cheddar cheese, shredded
1 medium onion, finely chopped
1/4 cup butter, melted
1 teaspoon salt
1/2 teaspoon black pepper

Preheat oven to 350 degrees. Combine all of the above ingredients _except_ the hash browns and mix thoroughly. Add hash browns and mix thoroughly. Pour in a greased 9 x 13 inch baking dish. Sprinkle with Topping* and bake _uncovered_ in preheated oven for 45 minutes.   Makes 10 servings
*Topping:
Mix together **2 cups crushed corn flakes and 1/4 cup melted butter.**

STUFFED VIDALIA ONIONS

6 Vidalia onions
1-1/2 cups Cheddar Cheese, grated
3 tablespoons butter

1/4 teaspoon salt
1/8 teaspoon pepper

Preheat oven to 350 degrees. Peel onions. Cut a slice off the top and core 3/4 down the inside center of each. Scoop out the center and chop, combining with grated cheese, salt & pepper. Divide the mixture evenly between the onions. and dot with butter. Place in a baking dish with a little water covering the bottom of the onions. Bake, covered, in preheated oven for about 1 hour until fork-tender. Uncover and bake 5 more minutes to brown.

Old Fashioned Macaroni & Cheese

8 ounce package elbow macaroni (makes 4 cups, cooked)
3 tablespoons butter
8 ounces sharp Cheddar cheese, grated
1 large egg
1-3/4 cups milk

Preheat oven to 325 degrees. Cook macaroni in salted water till tender. Drain in colander, then run hot water through it to rinse well. Arrange 1/3 of the macaroni in a greased 2 quart baking casserole dish, dot with 1/3 of the butter, sprinkle with 1/3 of the grated cheese. Repeat 2 more times. Beat egg and milk together and pour over macaroni. Do not stir. Press macaroni gently down with a fork till liquid comes up over the top. Add a little more milk, if necessary. Bake, uncovered, in preheated oven for 30 to 40 minutes till bubbly and golden brown. Makes 6 servings.

Macaroni & Cheese Deluxe

1 (8 ounce) package elbow macaroni, cooked
(10-3/4 ounce) can cream of mushroom soup
8 ounces sharp Cheddar cheese, grated
1/4 cup onions, chopped
1/4 cup bell pepper, chopped
1/4 cup pimiento, chopped
1 cup mayonnaise

Preheat oven to 350 degrees. Combine all of the above ingredients and place in a lightly greased 2 quart baking dish. Bake in preheated oven for 30 minutes. Makes 6 to 8 servings.

Tip: If you like *yellow* macaroni and cheese, add about 1/8 teaspoon paprika to the mixture.

FRIED GREEN TOMATOES

Mother had these often during the summer when she had an all-vegetable meal. With plenty of fresh vegetables available, her menu usually consisted of: tiny butterbeans, skillet-fried corn, (or corn-on-the cob), fried green tomatoes, sliced fresh tomatoes, fried squash with onions, fried eggplant and lots of crispy fried hoecake. She cooked her "big" meal at noon and friends or relatives just "happened" to drop by while she was cooking! And there was always enough to set "another place" for anyone who stopped by.

Large green tomatoes
1-1/2 cups all-purpose flour
1-1/2 cups plain cornmeal
1/2 teaspoon salt

1/2 teaspoon black pepper
Milk
Deep oil to fry

Wash tomatoes, cut off ends and slice into 1/2 inch slices. Mix flour, cornmeal, salt and pepper together and add just enough milk to make a thick batter. Heat oil in large skillet about 2 inches deep. Dip each tomato slice into batter and place in hot oil. Cook on both sides, turning once. Place slices, standing up, in a colander. Put on a plate when ready to serve. The colander keeps them from becoming soft as they would if placed on paper towels. Serve hot.

MARINATED GARDEN TOMATOES

4 large tomatoes, sliced
1/3 cup vegetable oil
1/4 cup Red Wine vinegar
1/2 teaspoon salt

1/4 teaspoon black pepper
1 clove garlic, crushed
2 tablespoons parsley, chopped
1 tablespoon finely chopped onion

Slice tomatoes 1/2 inch thick and place in a bowl. Combine oil, vinegar, salt, pepper and garlic in a small jar or blender and mix well. Pour over tomatoes. Sprinkle parsley & onion on top. Cover and refrigerate about 2 hours or till ready to serve.

GREEN BEAN CASSEROLE

The original 1950's recipe

2 (10 ounce) packages frozen cut or French-style green beans
1 (10-3/4 ounce) can cream of mushroom soup, undiluted
3/4 cup milk
1 teaspoon Worcestershire sauce
Pinch black pepper
1 (2.8 ounce) can French Fried Onions

Preheat oven to 350 degrees. Grease a 1-1/2 quart baking dish. In a large saucepan, cook green beans according to package directions. Drain and return beans to pan. Stir in soup, milk, Worcestershire sauce and black pepper. Stir in _1/2_ can French Fried Onions. Spoon mixture into casserole and bake, uncovered, for 30 minutes. Top with remaining _1/2_ can onions and bake for 5 minutes more or until hot and bubbly. Makes 8 servings.

MARINATED CARROTS

Also known as "Copper Pennies"

2 pounds carrots, peeled, sliced, & cooked in salty water till
        tender; drain.
1 bell pepper, sliced
1 onion, sliced
MARINADE:
1 (10-3/4 ounce) can Campbell's Tomato Soup
1 cup sugar
1/2 cup Mazola oil
1/2 cup white vinegar
1 tablespoon prepared mustard

Pour the marinade over carrots, pepper and onion. Toss, cover and keep in refrigerator for at least 24 hours before serving. Keeps well in fridge for at least a week. Makes about 8 servings.

Spinach casserole

This recipe, in layers, is better to me, than the recipes where everything is mixed together. It's really good, even if you don't care for spinach.

1 (10 ounce) package frozen chopped spinach, thawed
1 (10-3/4 ounce) can cream of mushroom soup
1 small onion, chopped
1 cup shredded Cheddar cheese (sharp or mild)
1/4 cup butter, melted
1 cup seasoned Pepperidge Farm Corn Bread Stuffing Mix

Preheat oven to 350 degrees. Spray a 1 quart casserole baking dish with Pam. Squeeze out most of the water from the spinach and spread evenly in bottom of the casserole dish. Combine the soup, onion and cheese and spread evenly over the spinach. Combine the melted butter and stuffing mix and spread over the soup mixture. Bake, uncovered, in preheated oven for 30 minutes. Makes 4 to 6 servings

Broccoli casserole

2 (10 ounce) packages frozen chopped broccoli
1 (10-3/4 ounce) can cream of mushroom soup
1/2 cup mayonnaise
1/2 minced onion
1 cup sharp Cheddar cheese, grated
2 large eggs, beaten
1 roll package Ritz cracker crumbs

Preheat oven to 400 degrees. Cook broccoli in boiling salted water 5 minutes. Drain. Mix soup, mayonnaise, onion cheese, eggs and broccoli together. Put in buttered 1-1/2 quart baking dish and sprinkle the cracker crumbs on top. Bake in preheated oven 20 minutes. Makes 8 servings.

Asparagus Casserole

1 (15 ounce) can cut asparagus, drained
1/2 teaspoon salt
1 teaspoon black pepper
1 (4 ounce) jar diced pimientos, drained
2 large eggs, beaten
1 cup Ritz cracker crumbs
1 cup milk or half & half
1 cup shredded Cheddar cheese
1/4 cup butter, melted

Preheat oven to 400 degrees. Mix everything together and pour into greased 8 inch square baking dish. Bake in preheated oven, *uncovered,* for 30 minutes.   Makes 6 servings
NOTE: 1 roll package of Ritz crackers, crushed in a food processor is equal to about 1 cup.

Squash Casserole

2 pounds squash, sliced
   into 1/4 inch slices
1 medium onion, minced
2 large eggs, beaten
1 cup evaporated milk
2 tablespoons butter
Salt & pepper to taste

1 cup sharp Cheddar cheese, grated
2 cups crushed Ritz crackers, about 2 rolls

Cook squash till tender, 15 to 20 minutes, Drain well and mash with a potato masher. Add onion, eggs, milk, butter, salt & pepper, cheese and 1/2 of the cracker crumbs. Place in buttered 9 x 13 inch baking dish and top with rest of cracker crumbs. Preheat oven to 350 degrees and bake, uncovered, for 45 minutes till top is brown. Makes 8 servings.
NOTE: you can use 2, 10 oz. packages frozen squash.

Southwestern Squash Casserole

2-1/2 pounds yellow squash, sliced in rounds
4 large eggs
1/2 cup half & half or milk
1 pound Monterey Jack cheese, shredded
1 teaspoon salt
2 teaspoons baking powder
3 tablespoons all-purpose flour
1 (4 ounce) can chopped green chilies
1-1/4 cups crushed corn chips, divided

Preheat oven to 350 degrees. Cook squash till tender, about 15 minutes; drain and cool. Combine eggs, half & half, cheese, salt, baking powder, flour and chilies, mixing well. Carefully stir in squash, keeping rounds in tack. Sprinkle *1/2* of the corn chips into the bottom of a greased 9 x 13 inch baking dish. Spoon the squash mixture over chips and top with the other half of the corn chips. Bake in preheated oven for 30 minutes. Makes 8 servings.

Corn Casserole with Cornbread

1/2 cup butter, melted
1 (8.5 ounce) package "Jiffy" corn muffin mix
1 (15 ounce) can whole kernel corn, drained
1 (14.75 ounce) can cream style corn
1 cup sour cream

Preheat oven to 350 degrees. Combine butter, corn muffin mix, both cans corn and sour cream, mixing well. Pour into a greased 8 or 9 inch square baking dish. Bake in preheated oven for 45 minutes or until golden brown. Makes 8 servings.
Optional: You can sprinkle 1 cup shredded sharp Cheddar cheese on top and return to oven for 15 more minutes to melt cheese.

SCALLOPED POTATOES AU GRATIN

I made this a lot in the '50's. It's a good accompaniment to a meat dish that doesn't have gravy. Example: Salmon Croquettes,, Fried Pork Chops, Meatloaf, etc.

2 tablespoons butter	2 cups milk
2 tablespoons flour	4 cups thin sliced potatoes
2 teaspoons salt	1/4 cup onion, chopped
1/8 teaspoon black pepper	1 cup sharp cheese, grated

Melt butter in a large saucepan; blend in flour. Add milk slowly and cook until thickened. Add salt and pepper. Place *1/2* of the sliced potatoes and onions in a greased 2 quart baking dish. Cover with *1/2* of the sauce. *Repeat layers.* Cover and bake in a preheated 350 degree oven for 45 minutes or until potatoes are fork-tender. Then remove cover and let top brown, 5 or 10 minutes. Makes 4 to 6 servings.

NOTE: For color you can add diced green bell pepper or pimiento to the potatoes before putting in casserole. And for a "one-dish" meal, put cubes of cooked ham in the layers after the potato layer. All you need is a tossed salad or green vegetable.

SPECIAL MASHED POTATOES

4 yellow Yukon Gold potatoes	2 large eggs, beaten
1 (8 ounce) package cream cheese, softened	1 tablespoon flour
	1/4 teaspoon salt
1 small onion, finely chopped	1 /8 teaspoon pepper
1/2 (6 ounce) can French-fried onions, crushed	

Preheat oven to 350 degrees. Cook potatoes in boiling salted water till tender, about 15 minutes; drain and mash. Add the rest of the ingredients, *except* crushed dried onions and beat with electric mixer. Spoon into 1-1/2 quart baking dish. Top with crushed dried onions and bake for 30 to 35 minutes.   Makes 4 servings.

TWICE BAKED POTATOES

6 large baking potatoes
1 cup sour cream
1/4 cup butter
Salt & pepper to taste
8 slices bacon, cooked & crumbled
1/4 cup chopped fresh chives
3 cups shredded Mozzarella cheese
1/2 cup shredded Swiss cheese

Preheat oven to 350 degrees. Cut a slice off top of each baked potato, lengthwise. Scoop out pulp leaving an 1/8 inch shell. Mash potato pulp; sour cream, butter, salt & pepper. Mix well. Gently stir in bacon, chives, and Mozzarella cheese. Divide potato mixture evenly between the six shells and sprinkle Swiss cheese on top. Bake in preheated oven for about 25 minutes. Garnish tops with a few sprinkles of chopped chives. Makes 6 servings.

CRAB STUFFED BAKED POTATOES

4 large baking potatoes, baked
1/2 cup butter, melted
1/2 cup milk
4 teaspoons grated onion
1 cup sharp Cheddar cheese, grated
1 teaspoon salt
Black pepper to taste
1 (6-1/2 ounce) can crabmeat
1/2 teaspoon paprika

Preheat oven to 350 degrees. Cut baked potatoes in half lengthwise. Scoop out pulp leaving an 1/8 inch shell. Beat potato pulp, butter, milk, onion, salt and black pepper together till well mixed. Fold in cheese and crabmeat. Divide mixture between the 8 shells and sprinkle with paprika. Place in preheated oven for about 20 minutes to heat thoroughly. Makes 8 servings.

CORN CASSEROLE DELUXE

This unusual corn casserole has cheese and green chilies. Very delicious!

2 large eggs
1 (14.5 ounce) can cream style corn
1 (8 ounce) container sour cream
1/4 cup butter, melted
1 (15 ounce) can whole kernel corn, drained
1-1/2 cups shredded sharp Cheddar cheese
1/2 cup finely chopped onion
1 (4 ounce) can diced green chilies, drained
1 (8.5 ounce) package "Jiffy" corn bread muffin mix

Preheat oven to 350 degrees. Combine eggs, cream corn, sour cream and butter. Add whole kernel corn, cheese, onion and chilies, stirring lightly to mix. Stir in dry corn bread muffin mix just until moistened. Pour into a greased 2 quart baking dish. Bake in preheat oven for 1 hour and 15 minutes or until a knife inserted in cent comes out clean.   Makes 8 servings.

GRANDMA'S SUNDAY MASHED POTATOES

4 large baking potatoes
2 tablespoons butter
2 (3 ounce) packages cream cheese, softened
2/3 cup sour cream

1/4 cup milk
3/4 teaspoon salt
2 tablespoons butter
1/2 teaspoon paprika

Peel, cube and cook potatoes in salty water till fork-tender. Drain; add all remaining ingredients *except butter and paprika.* Beat with electric mixer till blended. Spoon into lightly greased 9 x 13 baking dish. Melt remaining 2 tablespoons butter and brush on top; sprinkle with paprika. Bake in preheated 350 degree oven, uncovered, for 30 minutes until hot.   Makes 8 servings.

SWEET POTATO CASSEROLE

1 (29 ounce) can sweet potatoes
1 cup sugar
2 large eggs
1/4 cup butter, melted
1/2 cup evaporated milk
1/2 teaspoon cinnamon

1/2 teaspoon nutmeg
1 teaspoon vanilla
1 cup "plumped" raisins
Miniature marshmallows

Preheat oven to 400 degrees. Mix all of the ingredients together *except* raisins & marshmallows, in electric mixer and beat until smooth. Then stir in the plumped raisins. Pour into a greased 2 quart baking dish. Bake in preheated oven for 20 minutes. Then add marshmallow on top and bake for 5 minutes more.
Makes 8 servings.
NOTE: You can double this recipe using a 40 ounce can of sweet potatoes (40 ounces is 4 cups).

An <u>*alternate*</u> topping (instead of marshmallows) is this :
Mix together:
1/3 cup self-rising flour
2/3 cup light brown sugar
Cut
1/3 cup butter
into flour/sugar.
Add: **3/4 cup chopped pecans**
Sprinkle this mixture over sweet potatoes before baking.
Some people call this "Pumpkin Crunch".

Ask Granny

Dear Granny, how do you "plump" raisins?
Answer: Put the raisins in a bowl of very hot water. Let stand for 15 minutes. Drain *well.* This softens them.

TURNIP GREENS WITH HAM HOCKS

Wash fresh turnip greens in several waters leaf by leaf to get rid of any trace of sand. Pick the most tender part of the leaf from the stem and place in a big pot (or crockpot) with a small amount of water. There will be water left on the greens from the washing. Sandwich big hunks of ham hocks in between layers of greens, sprinkling a *little* bit of salt on top of each layer as you add the meat. Cover the pot and simmer until greens are tender, about 2 hours. You really can't cook them too long. Just check to make sure the water doesn't cook out of them. Keep adding a little water, if necessary. When the greens are tender, remove the ham hocks and cut into pieces. With two knives, criss-crossed, cut the greens very fine. The liquid that is left is called "pot-likker". Serve with lots of hot buttered cornbread, page 50. Grandpa likes to eat his cornbread crumbled in pot-likker.

FRIED APPLES

4 medium yellow Delicious apples
1/3 cup butter
3/4 cup brown sugar, packed
1 tablespoon plus 1 teaspoon cornstarch

1/2 teaspoon cinnamon
1-1/2 cups water

Slice, but do not peel apples; place in heavy 10 inch skillet. Combine the butter, brown sugar, cornstarch and cinnamon together, mixing well. Toss with apples, stirring to coat all pieces.
Add water to skillet. Put lid on skillet and cook over medium heat 12 to 15 minutes till apples are fork-tender and sauce is thick, stirring occasionally. To serve, either spoon all in a medium size serving bowl or divide into 4 individual serving bowls, ladling 1/2 cup of sauce into each bowl.
NOTE: After the apples are tender, you can remove skillet from heat and add 2 tablespoons of apple liqueur (Applejack).

GRANDMA'S BLUE RIBBON CAKES

RECIPES:

Grandma Dee, 1935
(check out that hair bow!)

MOTHER'S 18 LAYER CHOCOLATE CAKE

My mother and my husband had an on-going fun relationship. They were always teasing each other. This 18 layer cake was one of Mother's specialties, she was so proud of it. Once she baked it for Emery, brought it to our house, *proudly* gave it to him and left. He counted the layers and discovered there were only _17_! He promptly took it back to her and *demanded* his other layer! He never let her forget that she owed him that other layer!

1 cup Crisco shortening
2 cups sugar
6 large eggs
3 cups self-rising flour

1 cup sweet milk
2 teaspoons vanilla
1 teaspoon butter flavoring

Preheat oven to 350 degrees. Cream shortening and sugar. Add eggs, one at a time, beating well after each addition. Add flour to egg mixture, _alternately,_ with milk. Add flavorings. Grease the _backs_ of 9 inch cake pans and spread about 2 or 3 tablespoons of the batter on each. You'll have to do this 18 times. Bake in pre-heated oven for about 5 minutes. *Watch closely*. Repeat until all of the batter is gone and you have 18 layers.

FROSTING:

1/2 cup butter or margarine
2 squares unsweetened chocolate
1/2 cup sweet milk
1/4 cup light corn syrup

2 cups sugar
Dash of salt

Mix all ingredients together. Cook in a heavy saucepan till it reaches the soft ball stage, about 4 or 5 minutes. Spread between layers and on top, letting it run down the sides.

Mother once told me, "when you start to bake something, put all of the ingredients out on the counter before you start. Then as you use each thing, put it away. If you have anything left over, you've left something out!"

CREAM OF COCONUT CAKE

1 (18.25 ounce) package Duncan Hines French Vanilla cake mix
2 large egg whites
1-1/3 cups water
1 cup flaked coconut

Preheat oven to 350 degrees. Combine all of the above ingredients and beat on medium speed with electric mixer for 2 minutes. Reduce speed to low and beat for 1 minute more. Pour batter into greased and waxed paper lined 9 x 13 inch baking pan. Bake for 25 minutes. Cool in pan for 5 minutes. Turn out on wire cooling rack and peel off paper.
Place on serving plate (the 9 x 13 Tupperware cake carrier is good for this).
Make a foil "collar" all around cake, about 2 or 3 inches wide. Put just a little under the cake and let the rest lay over the sides. Prick the cake all over with tines of a fork. Combine the following and pour on top of cake. It will run "all over the place". This is why you put the foil all around the cake!

1 (14 ounce) can Eagle Brand sweetened condensed milk
1 (15.25 ounce) can crushed pineapple, *well drained*
1 (8-1/2 ounce) can Cream of Coconut

Next: Spread **a 12 ounce container of Cool Whip** evenly over top and around sides of the cake.
Gently pat **1 cup flaked** into the Cool Whip.
Cover and refrigerate for at least 4 hours .
When ready to serve cut into 12 to 15 squares.

Note: I leave the foil on it until I'm ready to cut it. The longer it has to chill, the better. When ready to serve, carefully remove the foil and cut into the serving size squares.

COCA-COLA CAKE

A fun and popular southern cake!

2 cups all-purpose flour
2 cups sugar
1 cup butter
3 tablespoons cocoa powder
1 cup Coca-Cola

1 teaspoon baking soda
1/2 cup buttermilk
2 large eggs, beaten
1 teaspoon vanilla
1-1/2 cups miniature
       marshmallows

Preheat oven to 350 degrees. Sift flour and sugar together in a mixing bowl. Heat butter, cocoa powder, Coca-Cola to the boiling point. Pour over flour/sugar mixture and mix well. Dissolve baking soda in buttermilk and add to mixture along with eggs and vanilla. Beat well. Stir in marshmallows. Batter will be thin. Pour into a greased 9x13 inch baking pan and bake in preheated oven for 40 to 45 minutes.

While still hot spread with this icing:
ICING:
1/2 cup butter or margarine, melted
3 tablespoons cocoa powder
6 tablespoons Coca-Cola
1 pound box powdered sugar, sifted
1 cup pecans, chopped

In a medium saucepan combine butter, cocoa powder and Coca-Cola. Bring to a boil, stirring constantly., boil for 3 minutes. Remove from heat and add powdered sugar, beating until smooth. Add pecans. Pour over cake while icing and cake are both still hot.

CHOCOLATE KAHLUA CAKE
ADDICTIVE!!!

CAKE:
1 (18.25 ounce) package Duncan Hines chocolate cake mix
1 (3.5 ounce) package instant chocolate pudding mix
1/2 cup vegetable oil
4 large eggs
3/4 cup strong brewed coffee
3/4 cup Kahlua liqueur

Preheat oven to 350 degrees. Combine all cake ingredients with
an electric mixer and beat at medium speed until well blended.
Pour into greased and floured 9 x 13 inch baking dish. Bake in preheated oven for about 45 minutes. Test with a straw for doneness. Mix glaze ingredients (below) together. While cake is still
warm, poke holes evenly all over the top and pour glaze mixture
over it. Cut in 15 squares and serve with Cool Whip and a cherry
on top!.

GLAZE:
1 cup sifted confectioners' sugar
2 tablespoons strong brewed coffee
1/4 cup Kahlua liqueur

Mix all together and following directions above.

Granny's Tip:

After pouring cake batter into pans, lightly
tap pan on the countertop several times to
take air out and make layers even.

MOCHA FUDGE CAKE

The combination of coffee, chocolate and sour cream make this a wonderfully moist and delicious cake.

1 cup boiling water
1 tablespoon instant coffee powder
2 squares unsweetened chocolate, cut into pieces
2 cups sifted cake flour
1/4 teaspoon salt
1 teaspoon baking soda
1/2 cup butter, softened
2 teaspoons vanilla
1-3/4 cups light brown sugar, firmly packed
2 large eggs
1/2 cup sour cream

Preheat oven to 325 degrees. Combine boiling water, instant coffee powder and chocolate in a small bowl. Stir until chocolate melts; cool. Sift flour; measure and resift with salt and baking soda; set aside. Beat butter, vanilla, brown sugar and eggs together at high speed until light and fluffy, about 5 minutes. Mix in flour mixture and sour cream *alternately* at low speed. Add chocolate mixture; mix at low speed just until blended. Spoon into a greased and floured paper-lined 9 x 9 x 2 inch baking dish. (or 8 x8 x 2) Bake in preheated oven for 1 hour. Cool in pan for 15 minutes then remove to wire cake rack to finish cooling. Frost with frosting below.

FROSTING:

Melt over low heat: **1 square unsweetened chocolate and 1 table-spoon butter.** Remove from heat, add *very slowly.* **1/2 cup sugar,** stirring constantly. Stir in slowly: **1/4 cup whipping cream** Bring **slowly** to a boil. Remove from heat, add: **1 square unsweetened chocolate,** stirring until melted. Add **1 teaspoon vanilla.** Cool to room temperature. Will be runny but thickens as it cools.

MISSISSIPPI MUD CAKE

We sold this in squares in our Home Sweet Home bakery. It was a great seller.

CAKE:

2 cups sugar	1-1/2 cups cake flour
1 cup butter	1/2 cup cocoa powder
4 large eggs	1/4 teaspoon salt
3 teaspoons vanilla	1 cup pecans, chopped

Preheat oven to 325 degrees. Cream sugar and butter together. Add eggs and vanilla, beating well. Sift the flour, cocoa and salt together. Add to creamy mixture. Stir in nuts. Pour into well greased and floured 9 x 13 baking pan. Bake in preheated oven for 30 to 35 minutes or until done when tested with toothpick.

Remove cake from oven and while cake is still hot, place **1 pound package miniature marshmallows** over cake to cover top.

While cake is cooling (about 20 minutes) make the icing.
ICING:

1 pound box powdered sugar	1/2 cup evaporated milk
1/3 cup cocoa powder	1 teaspoon vanilla
3/4 cup butter, melted	1 cup pecans, chopped

Sift sugar and cocoa together. Mix well with butter. Add milk, vanilla and nuts. When cake is completely cooled, pour icing on top of marshmallows in the pan. This cake will cut better if refrigerated for 2 hours. Makes 15 squares.

Ask Granny:

Dear Granny: The word "tad" is an old fashioned expression. Just how much is a "tad" of something?

Answer: A "tad" is like a "pinch" or a "dash". It varies in size depending on the taste of the "tadder".

Turtle Cake

CAKE:
1 (18.25 ounce) package German Chocolate Cake Mix
1-1/2 sticks butter
1-1/2 cups water
3 large eggs

Preheat oven to 350 degrees. Mix cake as directed on package of mix. Pour *1/2* of the batter in a greased and floured 9 x 13 inch baking pan. Bake in preheated oven for 15 minutes. Reserve the other half.

While the cake is baking:
In top of double boiler, over low heat melt:
1 (14 ounce) package caramels
Add:
3/4 cup margarine.
1/2 cup evaporated milk
Spread over cake.
Then combine the following and sprinkle over the caramel mixture:
1 (12 ounce) package chocolate chips
1 cup pecans, chopped
1 (7 ounce) can flaked coconut
Then pour the *other half of the cake batter* over that
Return to oven and bake for 30 minutes more.

FROSTING:

1 stick margarine	Dash of salt
1/3 cup milk	1 pound box powdered sugar
3-1/2 tablespoons cocoa	1 cup pecans, chopped

Bring margarine, milk, cocoa and salt to a boil over medium heat. Add sugar and nuts. Pour over cake while both are still hot.

6-LAYER CHOCOLATE CAKE

1 cup butter
2 cups sugar
4 large eggs
3 cups cake flour

1 teaspoon baking powder
1 cup milk
1 teaspoon vanilla

Preheat oven to 350 degrees. Cream butter and sugar together. Add eggs, one at a time, beating well after each addition. Sift cake flour and baking powder together. Add to egg mixture *alternately* with milk, beginning and ending with flour. Add vanilla. Pour into 6, 9 inch cake pans that have been lined with waxed paper and lightly greased. Bake in preheated oven for 10 to 15 minutes. Cool and frost with icing below.

ICING:

1 cup butter
4 tablespoons cocoa powder
3 cups sugar

1/2 cup milk
6 large marshmallows
1 teaspoon vanilla

Mix everything together *except* marshmallows and vanilla in sauce pan. Cook till softball stage, stirring constantly. Add marshmallows and vanilla. Beat and cool; spread between layers, on sides and top. If it starts getting hard to spread, dip knife in hot water and add to icing a few drops at a time.

Natalie
2000

Old Fashioned Chocolate Layer Cake

3/4 cup butter (1-1/2 sticks), softened
1-3/4 cups sugar
3 large eggs
2 teaspoons vanilla
2-3/4 cups cake flour
3/4 cup Hershey's cocoa powder
1-1/2 teaspoons baking soda
1/2 teaspoon salt
1-1/2 cups milk

Preheat oven to 350 degrees. Grease, flour and line 3, 9 inch round cake pans with waxed paper. In a large mixer bowl, beat butter till creamy; slowly add sugar, beating till light and fluffy, about 5 minutes. Add eggs, one at a time, beating well after each addition. Add vanilla; beat 1 minute. Sift dry ingredients together 3 times. Reduce speed to low and add flour mixture to bowl *alternately* in thirds with the milk, beginning and ending with flour, scraping sides of bowl. Divide batter evenly between the 3 pans and bake in preheated oven for 20 to 25 minutes, until toothpick inserted in center comes out clean. Cool pans on wire cake rack for 5 minutes, then remove from pans, peel off waxed paper. Cool completely. Frost with Divinity Icing on page 144

These 3 Grandmas are related; Barbara Allaert & Maggie Davis are sisters and Dianne Evans is their cousin. Taken Jan. 2001 in Punta Gorda, FL., celebrating Aunt Margaret's 90th Birthday.

WALDORF ASTORIA RED CAKE

The story goes that a lady, while visiting in New York City was dining at the famous Waldorf Astoria Hotel Restaurant. She ordered their delicious chocolate cake from the dessert menu. She loved the cake so much that when she got home she wrote the Chef, asking if she might have the recipe. He replied, sending her the recipe, along with a bill for $100. In the 1940's, $100 was a lot of money! Not only was it a surprise that he *even* charged her for the recipe, but charging a large amount like $100 was outrageous! She reported the incident to the newspapers, they printed the recipe and it became the rage all across the country, known as the $100 cake and the Waldorf Astoria Red Cake.

1 teaspoon baking soda	2 teaspoons cocoa powder
1 teaspoon white vinegar	2-1/2 cups cake flour
1/2 cup shortening	1 teaspoon salt
1-1/2 cups sugar	1 cup buttermilk
2 large eggs	1 teaspoon vanilla
2 ounces red food coloring	

Preheat oven to 350 degrees. Mix baking soda and vinegar together; set aside. Cream shortening and sugar together. Add eggs; beat well. Make a paste of the food coloring and cocoa and add to shortening mixture. Stir flour and salt together and add *alternately* with buttermilk. Mix in vanilla and baking soda-vinegar mixture. Pour into 2 greased and floured 8 inch round cake pans and bake in preheated oven for 30 minutes. When completely cool, slice each layer in half, making 4 layers. Frost between layers, sides & top.

FROSTING:

1-1/4 cups milk	1-1/4 cups sugar
5 tablespoons flour	1 tablespoon vanilla
1-1/4 cups butter	

Cook milk and flour until thick; cool. Cream butter and sugar till fluffy; add to milk mixture, beating constantly. Mix in vanilla and spread on cooled cake.

ORANGE SHERBET CAKE

1 (18.25 ounce) package orange cake mix
1 (3 ounce) package orange gelatin
1 cup water
1/3 cup vegetable oil
2 large eggs
1 teaspoon vanilla
1 teaspoon orange extract

Preheat oven to 350 degrees. Combine all of the above ingredients, beating well with electric mixer. Pour into 2 well greased and floured 9 inch cake pans. Bake in preheated oven for 30 minutes. When cool, cut each one in half, making 4 layers.

FILLING:

1 (16 ounce) container sour cream
2 cups sugar
1 (12 ounce) package flaked coconut
1/3 cup orange juice

1 teaspoon vanilla
1 teaspoon orange extract

Mix all filling ingredients together, _reserving 1 cup_. Put the rest of the filling between the 4 layers.
Mix the _reserved 1 cup_, with **1, 16 ounce container of Cool Whip**. Spread this mixture on the sides and top of cake.

Shirley E. Smith

Megan at Valdosta Arts & Crafts show selling Grandma Dee's dessert mixes. 1999

7-UP CAKE

1 (18.25 ounce) package Duncan Hines lemon cake mix
1 (3.4 ounce) package instant pineapple pudding & pie filling
3/4 cup Wesson oil
4 large eggs
1 cup 7-UP beverage

Preheat oven to 300 degrees. Beat oil and eggs together. Blend in mixes and stir in 7-UP. Divide evenly between 3 greased and floured 9 inch cake pans. Bake in preheated oven for 30 minutes.

ICING:

2 large eggs, lightly beaten	1/2 cup butter
2 tablespoons all-purpose flour	1 cup coconut
1-1/2 cups sugar	1 cup nuts, chopped (op.)
1 (8 ounce) can crushed pineapple, with juice	

Combine beaten eggs, flour and sugar, mixing well. Add rest of the ingredients and cook over medium heat until thickened. Cool; frost between layers, sides and top.

These four Grandmas, best friends in High School, are shown here at their 50th High School Reunion, Dec. 2000.
Joy Lewis Jones, Dianne Cooper Evans, Joyce White King and Dolores Stewart Herring.

Vanilla Wafer Cake

1 cup butter, softened
2 cups sugar
6 large eggs
1 teaspoon vanilla
1 (12 ounce) box vanilla wafers, *crushed*
1/2 cup milk
1 (7 ounce) package flaked coconut
1 cup chopped pecans

Preheat oven to 300 degrees. Cream butter and sugar till light and fluffy. Add eggs, one at a time, beating well after each addition. Stir in vanilla. Add vanilla wafers crumbs *alternately* with milk. Fold in coconut and pecans. Pour into a greased and floured 10 inch tube pan and bake in preheated oven for 1 hour and 30 minutes. Test with a straw to be sure it's done. Turn out on wire cake cooling rack and let cool completely. Make the glaze below:

GLAZE:
2 cups sugar
1 cup orange juice
1 tablespoon lemon juice

Combine all ingredients in sauce pan. Heat over low heat, stirring constantly. Do not let it boil. Pour hot glaze over cake.

Ask Granny:

Dear Granny: When a recipe calls for "sifted flour " or "flour sifted", what's the difference? **Answer:** When a recipe says "sifted flour" it means to *sift first* and then measure. When it says "flour sifted", it means to *measure first* and then sift.

Banana Split Cake

2 cups graham cracker crumbs
1/2 cup butter
2 cups powdered sugar
1 cup butter
2 large eggs
5 bananas
1 tablespoon lemon juice

1 (20 ounce) can crushed
   pineapple, drained
1 (12 ounce) carton Cool
   Whip
Hershey's chocolate syrup
1 cup chopped nuts
15 maraschino cherries

Mix graham cracker crumbs and 1/2 cup butter together; spread evenly in a 9 x 13 baking dish. Beat the powdered sugar, butter and eggs together for 15 minutes with electric mixer and pour over crust. Slice bananas and pour lemon juice over them so they won't turn dark. Place over butter mixture. Spread the drained pineapple over the bananas. Spread Cool Whip over pineapple. Dribble chocolate syrup over Cool Whip and sprinkle nuts on top. Decorate with cherries. Refrigerate until ready to serve, preferably overnight. Makes 15 servings

Lemon Pudding Pound Cake

4 large eggs, beaten
1 cup milk
3/4 cup cooking oil

1 (18.25 ounce) package Lemon
   Supreme Cake Mix
1 (3.5 ounce) instant lemon
   pudding & pie filling mix

Preheat oven to 325 degrees. Mix eggs, milk and oil together. Add the 2 mixes; beat 3 minutes. Pour in greased & floured tube pan and bake for 1 hour. Remove hot cake from pan, prick holes in top and pour glaze (below) over cake Makes 16 servings

GLAZE:
Combine **2 cups sifted powdered sugar** and **2 to 3 tablespoons lemon juice**; pour over hot cake.

Sour Cream Pound Cake

3 sticks butter (1-1/2 cups)
3 cups sugar
6 large eggs
3 cups cake flour

1/4 teaspoon baking soda
1 cup sour cream
1 teaspoon vanilla

Preheat oven to 325 degrees. Cream butter and add sugar a little at a time and beat until light and fluffy. Add eggs, one at a time, beating well after each addition. Sift flour with baking soda; add *alternately*, with the sour cream, beginning and ending with flour. Add vanilla and beat on low speed for 2 minutes. Pour into greased and floured tube pan and bake in preheated oven for 1 hour and 20 minutes.   Makes 16 servings

Cold Oven Pound Cake

A 1950's creation.

1 cup Crisco shortening
3 cups sugar
5 large eggs
1 cup milk

3 cups all-purpose flour
1 teaspoon baking powder
2 teaspoons vanilla
1 teaspoon lemon extract

Cream shortening and sugar together till light and fluffy. Beat in eggs, one at a time. Sift flour with baking powder; add *alternately* to creamed mixture *alternately* with milk. Stir in the flavorings. Spoon batter into greased and floured 10 inch tube pan. Place in *cold oven*. Turn oven on to 350 degrees and bake cake for 1 hour and 30 minutes. Turn out on cake rack to cool.
Makes 16 servings

Granny Says:

When mixing a pound cake, alternating flour and milk, always begin & end with the flour. And **always** read a recipe all the way through before starting to bake.

CREAM CHEESE POUND CAKE

This makes a big, beautiful cake and may become your favorite pound cake!

3 sticks butter (1-1/2 cups), softened
1 (8 ounce) package cream cheese, softened
3 cups sugar
6 large eggs
3 cups sifted cake flour
Dash of salt
1-1/2 teaspoons vanilla

Preheat oven to 325 degrees. Cream butter and cream cheese together, getting out all of the lumps. Gradually add sugar, beating till light and fluffy. Add eggs, one at a time, beating well after each addition. Add cake flour and salt. Stir in vanilla. Spoon batter into greased and floured 10 inch tube pan. Tap on the counter to remove any air bubbles. Bake in preheated oven for 1 hour and 30 minutes. Cool in pan 10 minutes. Then remove to cake rack to cool. Makes 16 servings

LYNN CLARK'S HERSHEY BAR CAKE

8 Hershey's Milk Chocolate Bars
    (1.55 ounces each)
2 cups Hershey's chocolate syrup
2 teaspoons vanilla
1 cup butter

2 cups sugar
4 large eggs
1/2 tsp. baking soda
2-1/2 cups cake flour
1 cup buttermilk

Preheat oven to 350 degrees. Melt candy bars and chocolate syrup in top of double boiler. Add vanilla and cool. Cream butter and sugar; add eggs, one at a time. Add chocolate mixture and beat. Combine baking soda and flour and add to above mixture *alternately,* with buttermilk. Pour in greased & floured tube pan and bake in preheated oven for 1 hour and 30 minutes.

Mother's "Secret" Pound Cake

Mother gave me this recipe and *swore* me to secrecy!
I always baked this in one of those long 15 inch loaf pans. Makes a great presentation and something different to take to potlucks!

2-3/4 cups sugar
2 sticks (1 cup) margarine
1 cup Crisco shortening
6 large eggs
1-1/4 cups evaporated milk
3 cups cake flour
2 teaspoons vanilla
1 cup chopped pecans

Mother, 1950's

Preheat oven to 300 degrees. Cream sugar, margarine and Crisco together, beating well until fluffy. Add eggs, milk and flour *alternately,* beating well after each addition. Add vanilla and nuts last and beat well. **Take out 1/2 cup of the cake batter and reserve.** This will go in the icing. Spoon cake in greased and floured 10 inch tube pan and bake in preheated oven for 1 hour and 30 minutes.

ICING:
1 cup evaporated milk
2 cups sugar
Reserved 1/2 cup cake batter
1 "lump" of butter (about 1 tablespoon)

Cook milk and sugar until it forms a hard ball. (test in a little bit of cold water. If it holds together in a little ball, it's done) Cool; then add the *reserved cake batter* and butter. Beat real hard until creamy. Pour over cake and let run down sides.

SOUR CREAM-COCONUT LAYER CAKE

This cake takes 3 days to "age". It's a favorite holiday cake in
North Carolina.

1 (18.25 ounce) package butter flavored cake mix
2 cups sugar
1 (16 ounce) carton sour cream
2 (6 ounces each) packages frozen coconut, thawed
1-1/2 cups Cool Whip

Prepare cake mix according to directions on package for 2,
8 inch layers. Bake; cool. When cool, split each layer in half,
making 4 layers. Combine sugar, sour cream and coconut, mix
well. Chill. *Reserve 1 cup* of this mixture for icing. Spread remaining
mixture *between* cake layers. (not on top or sides)
Combine reserved sour cream mixture with Cool Whip, stirring till
smooth. Spread on sides and top of cake. Seal in air tight container and refrigerate *3 days before serving.*

SHIRLEY'S BLUEBERRY CAKE

1 (18.25 ounce) package Duncan Hines Deluxe White Cake Mix
1 (12 ounce) container Cool Whip
1 (8 ounce) package cream cheese, softened
1/2 cup sugar
1/2 cup powdered sugar
1 (21 ounce) can Blueberry Pie Filling

Bake the cake mix as directed on package, in 3, 9 inch layers.
(350 degrees for 20 minutes) Cool. Mix the Cool Whip, cream
cheese and 2 sugars together. Then *alternate:* cake layer, Cool
Whip mixture and pie filling.
 NOTE: Put *1/2* of the pie filling on the first layer and the *rest* on
the 2nd layer. (**not** *on top*) "Frost" the top and sides with the
Cool Whip mixture.

142

OLD FASHIONED LEMON-CHEESE CAKE

One of Granny's specialties!

3 cups cake flour	3/4 cup milk
3 teaspoons baking powder	1/4 cup water
1/4 teaspoon salt	1 teaspoon lemon extract
1-1/2 cups sugar	1/2 teaspoon almond extract
1/2 cup shortening	3 large egg whites

Preheat oven to 350 degrees. Sift flour, baking powder and salt together *3 times*. Cream sugar and shortening together until light and fluffy. Combine milk and water. Add flour mixture and milk mixture *alternately*, beginning and ending with flour. Beat for 2 minutes or until batter is smooth. Add flavorings and beat 1 minute more. In separate bowl beat egg whites till stiff and carefully *fold* into cake batter. Pour into 2, 9 inch greased and floured cake pans and bake in preheated oven for 25 to 30 minutes.

FILLING:

1 cup sugar	1 teaspoon grated lemon rind
1/4 cup all-purpose flour	2 large egg yolks, beaten
1/4 teaspoon baking soda	Juice of 2 lemons
1-1/2 cups cold water	1 tablespoons butter

Mix sugar, flour and baking soda. Add water and lemon rind. Cook over low heat until thick. Add egg yolks, lemon juice and butter; cook for 2 minutes. Cool. Put filling between layers, on sides and top.

Optional: you can add a 3.5 ounce can of flaked coconut to filling, if desired.

"Granny, you got any MORE dolls?"   Marissa, 1984

GRANNY'S FAVORITE ICINGS

DIVINITY ICING

2-1/2 cups sugar	1/4 teaspoon salt
1/2 cup corn syrup	2 egg whites, stiffly beaten
1/2 cup hot water	1/2 teaspoon vanilla extract

Combine sugar, syrup, water and salt. Cook to soft ball stage (234-240 degrees, See page 127). Pour _1/2_ of the syrup over the stiffly beaten egg whites, beating constantly. Cook remaining syrup to hard ball stage(250-268 degrees); pour over egg whites, add extract; beat until spreading consistency. Do not make this on a rainy or cloudy day. Frosts a 2-layer 9 inch cake. Use this for Chocolate Cake or Devils Food Cake

MOTHER'S 7 MINUTE ICING

2 egg whites	1-1/2 cups sugar
1/4 teaspoon salt	1/3 cup water
2 teaspoons light corn syrup	1 teaspoon vanilla

Combine first 5 ingredients in top of double boiler. Beat 1 minute with electric mixer till well combined. Then cook, over simmering water, beating constantly about 5 minutes. Add vanilla and beat 1 minute more. Frosts a 2-layer 9 inch cake.
Note: I use this for Coconut Layer Cake.

AMARETTO-PECAN GLAZE FOR POUND CAKE

Combine in a small saucepan and bring to a boil:

1/4 cup plus 2 tablespoons butter	3/4 cup sugar
3 tablespoons Amaretto liqueur	3 tablespoons water

Boil for 3 minutes, exactly (time!), stirring constantly. Remove from heat and add **1 cup chopped pecans**. Pour over pound cake.

LEMON CUSTARD CAKE

It's different!

CUSTARD:
6 large egg yolks
3/4 cup sugar
3/4 cup lemon juice
1-1/2 teaspoons lemon rind
1 tablespoon plain gelatin
1/4 cup cold water
6 large egg whites
3/4 cup sugar
1 large 10 inch store-bought angel food cake

Combine the egg yolks, 3/4 cup sugar, lemon juice and lemon rind in top of a double boiler and cook until thickened. Dissolve gelatin in cold water; add to custard and cool in refrigerator. Then, beat egg whites and 3/4 cup sugar together: Fold into *cooled* custard. Grease a 2 quart mold or large glass bowl and pour some of the custard in the bottom. Tear the angel food cake into large pieces. Sprinkle some of the cake pieces over the custard. Repeat, alternating all of the custard and cake pieces. Chill well. When ready to serve, turn molded cake out onto a place and serve with whipped cream and chopped nuts. Makes 12 servings

FRESH COCONUT CAKE

Granny's favorite "Old Fashioned" Fresh Coconut Cake is a Duncan Hines White Cake Mix baked according to package directions in 2, 9 inch cake pans. Make "Mother's 7 Minute Icing" on page 144 and put *lots* of flaked coconut all over sides and top. Granny always hides her cake mixes in the back of her pantry. She doesn't want people to know *all* of her "secrets"!

CARROT-PINEAPPLE CAKE

2 cups cake flour
2 cups sugar
2 teaspoons baking soda
2 teaspoons cinnamon
1/2 teaspoon salt
3 large eggs, lightly beaten
3/4 cup salad oil
3/4 cup buttermilk

2 teaspoons vanilla
1 (8 ounce) can crushed
   pineapple, drained
2 cups carrots, grated
1 cup flaked coconut
1 cup pecans, chopped

Preheat oven to 350 degrees. Mix the flour, sugar, baking soda, cinnamon and salt together. Combine eggs, oil, buttermilk and vanilla together. Add to dry ingredients. Stir in drained pineapple, carrots, coconut and pecans. Pour into greased 9 x 13 inch baking pan. Bake in preheated oven for 45 to 55 minutes. Cool and top with frosting.

CREAM CHEESE FROSTING:
1/2 cup butter, softened
1 (8 ounce) package cream cheese, softened
1 pound box powdered sugar, sifted
1 cup pecans, chopped
1 teaspoons vanilla

Beat all ingredients together, except nuts, with electric mixer. Add nuts and frost cooled cake.

ALTERNATE FROSTING FOR CARROT CAKE

1 cup sugar
1/2 cup buttermilk
1 teaspoon baking soda

1 tablespoon light corn syrup
Dash salt

Put all ingredients in saucepan and cook till thickened, about 2 or 3 minutes. Frost cooled cake

Apricot Nectar Cake

1 (18.25 ounce) box Duncan Hines Lemon Supreme Cake Mix

1/2 cup sugar

3/4 cup vegetable oil

4 large eggs

1 cup apricot nectar

Preheat oven to 325 degrees. Put all ingredients in a large mixing bowl and beat until well mixed. Pour into a well greased 10 inch tube pan. Bake in preheated oven for 1 hour and 15 to 20 minutes. Test cake with straw to see if It's done. Turn out on cake cooler and pour the following topping over the _hot_ cake.

TOPPING: 1 cup sifted powdered sugar and 3 tablespoons lemon juice.

Italian Cream Cake

This is the original 1970's recipe.

2 cups sugar

1/2 cup shortening

1/2 cup butter

5 large eggs, separated

1 tablespoon vanilla

1 cup buttermilk

2 cups sifted all-purpose flour

1 teaspoon baking soda

2 cups flaked coconut

1 cup chopped pecans

Preheat oven to 350 degrees. Cream sugar and shortening together; add butter and beat until fluffy. Add the egg _yolks_, one at a time, beating well after each addition. Sift flour and baking soda together and add _alternately_ with the vanilla and buttermilk. Add coconut and pecans. Beat egg _whites_ until stiff and fold in. Pour into 3 greased & floured 9 inch cake pans. Bake in preheated oven for 30 minutes. Cool and frost.

CREAM CHEESE FROSTING:.

8 ounce package cream cheese, softened

1/2 cup butter, softened

1 teaspoon vanilla

4 cups powdered sugar

1 cup chopped pecans

Beat cream cheese and butter until light & fluffy. Add vanilla and sugar; beat until creamy. Spread between layers, sides and top of cooled cake. Sprinkle pecans evenly over top of cake.

PINEAPPLE-COCONUT CAKE

A real show-stopper....when Granny wants to show off!

3/4 cup butter	2-1/2 cups cake flour
1-1/2 cups sugar	3 teaspoons baking powder
4 large eggs	1 cup flaked coconut
1 cup crushed pineapple, with juice	1 teaspoon vanilla

Preheat oven to 350 degrees. Cream butter and sugar together till light and fluffy. Add eggs, one at a time, beating well after each addition. Add pineapple with juice. Sift cake flour and baking powder together and add slowly, to mixture in thirds. Add coconut and vanilla. Pour evenly into 3 greased and paper-lined 9 inch cake pans. Bake in preheated oven for about 25 minutes. Cool in pans for 5 minutes before turning out on wire cake coolers to finish cooling.

NOTE: *You need to purchase a 14 ounce bag of flaked coconut to have enough for the cake batter and assembling the cake.*

FILLING:

3 tablespoons flour

1/2 cup sugar

1/8 teaspoon salt

1 (20 ounce) can crushed pineapple, with juice

2 tablespoons butter

Combine in a medium saucepan and cook over medium heat, stirring constantly until thickened, about 15 minutes. Cool in freezer for about 10 minutes. This makes 2 cups of cooked filling.

ICING: "Mother's 7 Minute Icing". Make this while your filling is chilling in the freezer. You need the icing in order to assemble the cake.

ASSEMBLING; Place 1 layer, round side down on cake plate. Spread a thin layer of icing, thin layer of filling and sprinkle with coconut. Place 2nd layer round side up & *repeat*. Place 3rd layer round side up & repeat. Frost sides with remaining icing. Sprinkle coconut on sides of cake. Refrigerate for about 1 hour to set filling.

Fuzzy NAVEL CAKE
Just as good as the drink!

1 (18.25 ounce) package yellow cake mix
1 (5.1 ounce) package instant vanilla pudding & pie filling mix
4 large eggs, slightly beaten
1/2 cup applesauce
3/4 cup peach schnapps
1/2 cup orange juice

Preheat oven to 350 degrees. In a large bowl stir the cake mix and pudding mix together. In a separate bowl, by hand, stir together the eggs, applesauce, peach schnapps and orange juice. Stir into the cake/pudding mixture, mixing well. Pour into a greased, floured, and waxed paper lined or 10 inch tube pan. Bake in preheated oven for about 1 hour or until tested done with a straw.
GLAZE:
1/4 cup peach schnapps
2 tablespoons orange juice
1 cup sifted powdered sugar

Combine glaze ingredients together, beating until smooth. While cake is still warm, (do not remove from pan) poke holes in cake with fork tines. Pour hot glaze all over top. Let cake cool in pan at least 2 hours before removing.

PLUM EASY CAKE

2 cups self-rising flour
2 cups sugar
1 teaspoon cinnamon
1 cup chopped nuts

3 large eggs
1 cup vegetable oil
2 small jars baby food plums
1 teaspoon cloves

Preheat oven to 325 degrees. Mix all together and pour into well greased 10 inch tube pan. Bake for 1 hour and 15 minutes.

MANDARIN ORANGE CAKE

Great cake to take to covered dish suppers. In North Carolina, this is known as the "Pig Pickin' Cake".

1 (18.25 ounce) package Duncan Hines yellow cake mix
4 large eggs
1/2 cup vegetable oil
1 (11 ounce) can Mandarin oranges, with juice

Preheat oven to 350 degrees. Beat the cake mix, eggs, oil, oranges and juice together just until smooth. Pour into 3 well-greased and floured 9 inch cake pans. Bake in preheated oven for 25 minutes. Cool about 5 minutes before removing from pans. Remove from pans and finish cooling on wire cake racks. Then frost with the icing below.

ICING:
1 (3.4 ounce) package vanilla pudding & pie filling mix
1 (20 ounce) can crushed pineapple, drained
1 (12 ounce) carton Cool Whip

Place pudding mix in a bowl; add drained pineapple and mix well. Fold in Cool Whip, mixing just until blended. Ice cake and then refrigerate. Keep cake refrigerated between servings.

STRAWBERRY CAKE

1 (18.25 ounce) package white cake mix   1/2 cup water
3 teaspoons cake flour   1 cup salad oil
1 (3 ounce) package strawberry gelatin   4 large eggs
1 (10 ounce) package frozen strawberries, thawed

Preheat oven to 350 degrees. Mix the cake mix, cake flour, and gelatin together. In a separate bowl, combine _3/4 cup_ strawberries, water and oil together and add to cake mix mixture. Save rest of strawberries for frosting. With electric mixer add eggs, one at a time, beating well after each addition. Pour into in 3 greased and waxed paper lined 9 inch round cake pans. Bake in preheated oven for 35 minutes. Cool completely on wire cake racks and frost with frosting below.

FROSTING:

1 stick margarine   Enough thawed straw-
1 (16 ounce) box powdered sugar   berries to whip like cream
Pinch salt

Beat until creamy, then frost between layers, sides & top.

OATMEAL CAKE

1 cup rolled oats   1 teaspoon vanilla
1-1/4 cups boiling water   1-1/3 cups all-purpose flour
1/2 cup butter   1/2 teaspoon salt
1 cup brown sugar   1 teaspoon baking soda
1 cup white sugar   1 teaspoon cinnamon
2 large eggs, beaten   1/2 cup pecans, chopped

Preheat oven to 350 degrees. Pour boiling water over oats and let stand 20 minutes. Cream butter & sugars; mix with oats. Add eggs and vanilla. Sift dry ingredients together and add to creamed mixture. Add pecans and pour in greased & floured 9 x 13 inch baking pan. Bake for 30 to 35 minutes.

GRANNY'S BLACKBERRY WINE CAKE

Granny made great blackberry wine! Grandpa loved this cake, but he really preferred *drinking* the wine and eating the cake! Granny said a glass of her blackberry wine each night was very *medicinal* and would help a body sleep better.

1/2 cup chopped pecans
1 (18.25 ounce) package Duncan Hines white cake mix
1 (3 ounce) package blackberry gelatin
4 large eggs
1/2 cup vegetable oil
1 cup blackberry wine

Preheat oven to 325 degrees. Grease a 10 inch tube pan and pour pecans evenly in the bottom. In a large mixing bowl, combine the cake mix, gelatin, eggs, oil and blackberry wine together; beat for 2 minutes. Then pour in pan over pecans. Bake in preheated oven for 40 to 45 minutes or till tests done with a toothpick. While still warm, leaving it in the pan, carefully pour *1/2 cup* of the wine glaze (below) over top. Let set 10 minutes and then remove cake from pan. Cool completely on wire rack and then pour the remainder of the glaze on top. Spread with a metal spatula to distribute evenly   Makes about 16 servings.

WINE GLAZE:
1 cup sifted powdered sugar
1/2 cup blackberry wine
1/2 cup butter, softened

Mix the powdered sugar and wine together; add softened butter and beat until smooth.

Hat with Morgan!
1990

Banana Pecan Cake

2-1/2 cups cake flour
1-2/3 cups sugar
1-1/4 teaspoons baking powder
1-1/4 teaspoons baking soda
1 teaspoon salt
1-1/2 teaspoons cinnamon
3/4 teaspoon nutmeg
1/2 teaspoon cloves

2/3 cup shortening
2/3 cup buttermilk
1-1/4 cups mashed
    bananas
2 large eggs

Preheat oven to 350 degrees. Sift all of the dry ingredients together. Add shortening, buttermilk and bananas; beat on low speed for 2 minutes. Then add eggs and beat on low for 1 minute. Pour in greased 9 x 13 inch baking pan and bake for 45 minutes. NOTE: You can bake this in 2, 9 inch round cake pans for 35 minutes. Frost with the icing below.

ICING:
1/2 stick butter, melted
1 (16 ounce) package powdered sugar
1 large banana, mashed
1 cup pecans, finely chopped

Cream butter and sugar;
add banana and nuts.
Spread on cooled cake.

My parents,
Ralph & Shirley Cooper
1945

Grandma's Menus

Sunday Dinner with the Preacher

Years ago, the preacher and his family were always
invited for Sunday dinner with a member of the congregation.
Granny was always happy when it was her turn and she planned
one of her finest Sunday dinners!

Buttermilk Fried Chicken, p.93
Mashed Potatoes with Cream Gravy
Fresh Butterbeans
Turnip Greens with Ham Hocks, p. 122
Squash Casserole, 116
Garden Tomatoes, sliced
Grandma Dee's Yeast Biscuits, p. 49

Granny gets up very early and fries her chicken, cooks her
butterbeans and turnip greens before she goes to church. Her
squash casserole is ready to go into the oven when she returns.

She sets the table with her momma's hand-embroidered table-
cloth, her Sunday china and carefully places red roses from her
garden in the center of the table.

When she returns from church, she prepares her mashed potatoes and bakes her yeast biscuits while the squash casserole is
baking.

After dinner, Granny serves
coffee and her very special
dessert,
6-Layer Chocolate Cake, p 132
and vanilla ice cream.

*(after the preacher and his family
have gone, Granny and Grandpa
take a nap!)*

FARMHOUSE PIES

RECIPES:

Raymond & Tisha Cooper
Wedding Portrait
1903

ANN'S LEMON MERINGUE PIE

This is the very first pie given to me after I married...from Ann Groover Tucker in 1954. I made it often because it was so easy and so good.

3 large eggs, separated
1 (14 ounce) can Eagle Brand sweetened condensed milk
1/3 cup lemon juice
1 (9 inch) baked pie shell

Beat egg yolks with a fork; add condensed milk and beat with a large spoon till blended. Add lemon juice and stir till well mixed. Pour into cooled baked pie shell. Make meringue.

MERINGUE:
3 large egg whites
3 tablespoons sugar

Preheat oven to 350 degrees. Beat the egg whites till foamy; add the sugar, beating till stiff. Spread evenly on pie, with the back of a large spoon, making pretty swoops and sealing the edges. Bake in preheated oven for 15 minutes or until meringue is pretty and brown.

My Grandma, (Tisha Cooper) "Mama" with her namesake, my first-born, Tisha Dianne Evans, 1955

GRANDMA DEE'S FRIED PIES

A North Carolina country festival favorite!

PASTRY:

3 cups all-purpose flour

1 teaspoon salt

1 tablespoon sugar

3/4 cup Crisco

1 large egg, beaten

1/4 cup + 1 tablespoon cold water

1 teaspoon cider vinegar

Place flour, salt and sugar in a food processor and pulse once to stir. Break up shortening into large pieces and drop around flour mixture. In a small bowl, mix together the beaten egg, cold water and vinegar. Add to processor. Process, in quick pulses, just until it forms a ball. Remove and divide into 13 pieces. Roll out each piece, place a sauce over it and cut with a knife to make a 5 inch round piece. This dough doesn't have to chill.
Makes 13, 5 inch pies.

APPLE FILLING:

6 cups cooking apples, finely chopped

3/4 cup sugar

1 tablespoon vanilla

1/4 teaspoon nutmeg

1 tablespoon vanilla

1 tablespoon flour

2 tablespoons apple cider

1/2 teaspoon cinnamon

Combine all ingredients in a large saucepan and cook on *low*, covered, stirring frequently for about 30 minutes till apples are soft. Put about 3 tablespoons of filling on one side of each pastry. Moisten the edges with a little water and fold over in half; with a fork, dipped in flour, press around edges to seal. Make about 3 air vents on top. To fry pie, heat about one inch of vegetable oil to 375°. Fry pies till golden brown, turning once. Drain on paper towels. **OR** place on lightly greased baking sheet and bake in 400° oven for 15 minutes. **Icing:** make a mixture of **2 cups sifted confectioner's sugar, ½ teaspoon vanilla and about 2 tablespoons milk.** Drizzle over tops of cooled pies.

BEST APPLE PIE

8 cups cooking apples, peeled & thinly sliced
1/3 cup light brown sugar, firmly packed
1/3 cup granulated sugar
1 tablespoon cornstarch
1 teaspoon cinnamon
1-1/2 teaspoons apple pie spice
1/4 teaspoon salt
Pastry for double 9 inch pie crust
2 tablespoons butter

Preheat oven to 425 degrees. Place sliced apples in a bowl and let sit about 15 minutes till juice forms. Meanwhile mix the sugars, cornstarch, cinnamon, apple pie spice and salt together. Toss apples to coat and place in pie shell. Dot with butter. Roll out top crust and place over the filling, turning the edges under and flute. Cut 3 or 4 steam vents on top or use a decorative cookie cutter (apple cutter would be nice). Brush the top lightly with a little milk and sprinkle sugar on top. Bake at 425° for 45 minutes. Serve vanilla ice cream on side.

 Multiply this as many times as you wish and keep in an airtight jar:

Apple Pie Spice Mix:
2 teaspoons cinnamon
2 teaspoons nutmeg
1 teaspoon cardamom

These two 1-1/2 year –olds are now in their 40's! They were born on the same day and couldn't seem to "disconnect"!

Banana Split Pie

1 (15-1/2) ounce can crushed
    pineapple, drained
3/4 cup sugar
2 tablespoons flour
3 bananas, sliced

2 graham cracker crusts
1 cup coconut
1 cup pecans, chopped
1 (8 ounce) tub Cool Whip

Combine pineapple, sugar and flour in medium saucepan. Cook over low heat until thickened, stirring several times. Place sliced bananas evenly between the two pie crusts. Pour filling over bananas and sprinkle with coconut and pecans. Cover the top of the 2 pies with the Cool Whip, dividing evenly between the two. Refrigerate overnight. When ready to serve: drizzle a little chocolate syrup on top, sprinkle a few chopped nuts and top with a Maraschino cherry.

Dutch Apple Pie

3 cups cooking apples,
    peeled & sliced
1 (9 inch) unbaked pie shell
1 cup sugar
3 tablespoons flour
1/2 teaspoon cinnamon

1 large egg, beaten
1 cup light cream
1 teaspoon vanilla
1/2 cup chopped pecans
1 tablespoon butter
1/2 cup shredded cheese

Preheat oven to 350 degrees. Place the apples in pie shell. Mix the sugar, flour and cinnamon together. Combine egg, cream and vanilla and add to sugar mixture. Mix well and pour over apples. Sprinkle with chopped nuts and dot with butter. Bake for 45 to 50 minutes. Remove from oven and while still hot, sprinkle with cheese. Best served warm.

BANANA CREAM PIE

1 cup sugar	1 teaspoon banana extract
1/4 cup cornstarch	1 teaspoon vanilla
1/4 teaspoon salt	4 medium bananas, sliced
2 cups milk	6 tablespoons sugar
3 large eggs, separated	1 (9 inch) baked pie shell
1 tablespoon butter	*or* graham cracker pie shell

Combine sugar, cornstarch and salt in top of double boiler. Add milk gradually, stirring constantly. Cook over boiling water until thickened, stirring constantly. (this will take about 25 minutes) Beat the egg yolks in a small bowl until pale yellow. Add a little of the hot mixture, stirring to combine, then pour back into the double boiler with rest of hot mixture. Cook about 4 minutes more. Remove from heat and add butter and flavorings. Slice 2 of the bananas evenly in the bottom of the pie shell; pour 1/2 of the hot custard over. **Repeat layers.** Spoon meringue on top and bake at 350 degrees for 15 minutes. Cool completely before serving. Store in refrigerator between servings.

MERINGUE: Beat egg whites until foamy. Add the 6 tablespoons sugar, one tablespoon at a time, beating well after each addition till stiff peaks form.

Pie Tips:

#1 Meringue should always touch the crust all the way around to allow for shrinkage while baking.

#2. For a crisper *baked* pie shell, brush the pie shell with melted butter, sprinkle evenly with a little granulated sugar; prick the inside all over with a fork to prevent "puffing up". Then bake in a 425 degree oven for 9 to 10 minutes. Cool completely before filling.

PEANUT BUTTER CREAM PIE

This is a great pie. Even people who do not like peanut butter will ask you for the recipe! And you have to *tell* them it's peanut butter!

3/4 cup sifted powdered sugar
1/3 cup creamy-style peanut butter
1 (9 inch) baked pie shell
3 tablespoons cornstarch
3/4 cup sugar
1/8 teaspoon salt
2 cups milk
3 large eggs, separated
2 tablespoons butter
1 teaspoon vanilla
1/4 teaspoon cream of tartar
1 teaspoon cornstarch
2 tablespoons sifted powdered sugar

Combine 3/4 cup powdered sugar and peanut butter. Blend well with pastry cutter till it looks like coarse crumbs. Sprinkle *3/4 of the crumb mixture on the bottom of the baked pie shell, reserving the remainder of the crumbs.* Combine cornstarch, sugar and salt in top of double boiler. Over medium heat, gradually add milk and cook, stirring constantly, till thickened. Cover and cook 10 minutes more, stirring occasionally. Beat egg yolks slightly with a fork. Stir a small amount of hot mixture into yolks and then pour back into boiler, blending well. Cook 2 minutes more, stirring constantly. Remove from heat and gently stir in butter and vanilla. Set aside while preparing meringue.

MERINGUE: Beat egg whites, cream of tartar and cornstarch at high speed till foamy. Gradually add 2 tablespoons powdered sugar and beat till still. Pour custard into pie shell and top with meringue. Then sprinkle *reserved* peanut butter/sugar mixture on *top* of meringue. Bake at 350° for about 15 minutes till golden. It looks gorgeous and is well worth the effort.

FRESH BLACKBERRY PIE

Flossie picks a bucket full of blackberries so Grandma can bake her a pie.

3 cups fresh berries, washed
1 cup sugar
1/4 cup flour or minute tapioca
1/4 teaspoon salt
1/2 teaspoon cinnamon
1 tablespoon lemon juice
2 tablespoons butter
Pastry for double 9 inch pie crust

Preheat oven to 425 degrees. Combine berries, sugar, flour, salt, cinnamon and lemon juice, mixing well to coat berries. Pour into unbaked pie crust. Dot with butter. Cover with the top crust. At this point you could use a little cookie cutter to make the cut our vents or cut the top crust into 1/2 inch strips and make a pretty lattice top. If not, just cover with top pastry, crimp and make the steam vents as usual. Bake for about 40 minutes or until crust is brown.

Pie Tip:

To reduce fat, make a bottom crust only and choose a streusel topping (below) instead of a top crust.

Streusel Topping:
In a bowl, mix **1/2 cup light brown sugar**, firmly packed, **1/2 cup sifted all-purpose flour** and **1/2 teaspoon cinnamon**. With pastry blender, cut in **1/3 cup cold** butter until mixture is crumbly. Sprinkle evenly over pie and bake as directed.

FRESH BLUEBERRY PIE

1 cup sugar
3 tablespoons cornstarch
1 cup water
4 cups fresh blueberries
1 tablespoon butter
Pastry for double 9 inch pie crust

Preheat oven to 425 degrees. Combine sugar. cornstarch and water in large saucepan. Cook over medium heat till thickened and clear; add blueberries. Spoon into pie shell and dot with butter. Cover with top pastry, flute edge and make steam vents. Lightly brush with milk or water and sprinkle sugar on top. Bake for 40 minutes or until crust is golden brown.

NOTE: For a different taste, substitute light brown sugar for the granulated.

COCONUT CUSTARD PIE

4 large eggs	2 teaspoons vanilla
2/3 cup sugar	1 cup flaked coconut
1/2 teaspoon salt	Nutmeg
2-2/3 cups milk	1 (9 inch) unbaked pie shell

Preheat oven to 425 degrees. In a large mixer bowl beat first 5 ingredients together. Stir in coconut. Pour into pie shell and sprinkle with nutmeg. Bake at 425° for 15 minutes. Lower heat to 350° and bake for 25 to 30 minutes or until it tests done when knife is inserted into center. Let cool completely. Refrigerate 30 minutes before serving.

CHCOLATE CREAM PIE

Great old fashioned taste!

1-1/4 cups sugar

1/2 cup unsweetened cocoa

1/4 teaspoon salt

1/3 cup cornstarch

3 cups milk

3 large eggs, separated

3 tablespoons butter

1-1/2 teaspoons vanilla

1/4 teaspoon cream of
tartar

1/4 cup sugar

1 (9 inch) baked pie shell

Combine sugar, cocoa, salt and cornstarch in the top of a double boiler. Over *simmering* water, *gradually* add milk, stirring constantly until it thickens and comes to a boil. This will take about 10 minutes. Cook for 1 minute, stirring constantly. Beat 3 egg yolks with a fork till lemon colored. Stir 1/4 of the hot mixture into the egg yolks, then back into the boiler. Cook for 2 minutes, stirring constantly. Remove from heat and stir in butter and vanilla. Make meringue with the egg whites, cream of tartar and sugar. Pour chocolate filling into the cooled baked pie shell and top with meringue. Bake at 350° for 15 minutes till golden.

Ask Granny:

Dear Granny: What's the difference between a "*cream*" pie and a "*custard*" pie?
Answer: A "*cream*" pie filling is cooked on top of the stove and poured in an already baked pie shell. It's usually topped with meringue and put back into the oven to bake the meringue.
Example: Banana Cream Pie.

A "*custard*" pie filling is mixed together, poured into a raw pie shell and baked in the oven. It's usually served with whipped cream or Cool Whip. Example: Pumpkin Pie. Both kinds need to chill in the refrigerator before serving so they will slice better.

Coconut Cream Pie

1 cup sugar	1 teaspoon vanilla
1/4 cup cornstarch	1 teaspoon coconut extract
1/4 teaspoon salt	1-1/3 cups (3-1/2 ounce can)
2 cups milk	flaked coconut
3 large eggs, separated	1 (9 inch) baked pie crust
1 tablespoon butter	

Combine the sugar, cornstarch and salt in top of a double boiler. Over boiling water, stir in the milk slowly, stirring constantly with whisk till thickened, about 25 minutes. Beat egg yolks with a fork in a small bowl till lemon colored. Add a little of the hot mixture to the egg yolks; stir and then add to the rest of the hot mixture. Cook about 4 minutes, stirring constantly. Remove from stove and stir in butter, flavorings and coconut.

Meringue: 3 egg whites, 1/4 teaspoon cream of tartar and 6 tablespoons sugar. Spread over pie, carefully sealing the edges. Sprinkle a little **coconut** on top of the meringue and put in 350° oven for about 15 minutes, till golden brown.

Lemon Coconut Cream Pie

Follow the directions above for Coconut Cream Pie and when you remove thickened filling from stove, stir in the butter, flavorings and coconut. **Add 2 tablespoons fresh lemon juice.**

Note: For a baked pie crust, prick the unbaked pie shell all over with a fork and place in a preheated 450 degree oven. Bake for 9 or 10 minutes. Check after 9 minutes, it's probably long enough. After that it could burn very quickly.

EGG CUSTARD PIE

An old fashioned recipe

6 large eggs, lightly beaten
1 cup heavy cream
3/4 cup milk
4 tablespoons butter

1 cup sugar
1 teaspoon vanilla
Nutmeg
1 (9 inch) unbaked pie shell

Preheat oven to 400 degrees. Mix eggs, cream, milk, butter and sugar together in a large bowl. Set pie shell on oven rack and *then* pour filling into it. The filling will come right up to the top so put a cookie sheet on the *bottom shelf* to catch any drips. Sprinkle a little nutmeg on top. Very *carefully* slide back into oven. Bake at 400° for 10 minutes. Then reduce oven temperature to 350° and bake for 30 minutes. Makes a *beautiful* golden pie that will bring back *beautiful memories!*

SOUTHERN LEMON CHESS PIE

Delish!!

1 cup sugar
1 tablespoon flour
1 tablespoon yellow cornmeal
4 large eggs, beaten

1/3 cup lemon juice
1/4 cup milk
1/3 cup melted butter
1 (9 inch) unbaked pie shell

Preheat oven to 350 degrees. Combine sugar, flour and cornmeal. Add the beaten eggs and lemon juice, blending well. Stir in milk and melted butter. Pour into pie shell and bake for 45 minutes.

FRENCH SILK PIE

1/2 cup butter
3/4 cup sugar
2 large eggs
2 (1 ounce each) squares
  unsweetened chocolate, melted
1 teaspoon vanilla

1 (9 inch) baked pie shell
1/2 pint heavy cream
2 tablespoons sugar
1 tablespoon rum (op.)
Slivered almonds

Cream butter and sugar until very light and fluffy. Add eggs, one at a time, beating 2 minutes after each addition. Add cooled, melted chocolate and beat for 3 more minutes. Add vanilla, beating for 2 more minutes. Pour into baked pie shell and chill at least 4 hours till firm. This pie improves with age. It really tastes better when allow to chill for several days. If you can make it ahead, you'll have a much better dessert. When ready to serve, beat the heavy cream till soft peaks form, add 2 tablespoons sugar and the rum, if desired. (you can substitute vanilla extract for the rum.)

The Chocolate Whipped Cream below, is an optional topping. Spoon on top of pie and sprinkle with chocolate curls.

CHOCOLATE WHIPPED CREAM: Place electric beaters in **freezer.** Combine: **3 tablespoons unsweetened cocoa powder and 2 tablespoons confectioners' sugar.** Slowly add **1 cup heavy cream** and with wire whisk, stir until smooth. Then add **1 teaspoon vanilla.** With chilled beaters, beat on high until soft peaks form.

*P*ie *T*ip:

To mend cracks in pie crust and to seal folds in Pillsbury All-Ready pie crusts, wet fingers with cold water and press the edges together.

German Chocolate Pie

A 1950's Christmas favorite. This is the *original* recipe.

3 cups sugar
6 tablespoons unsweetened cocoa
Pinch of salt
4 large eggs
1 (12 ounce) can evaporated milk
1 teaspoon vanilla
1/2 cup butter, melted
2 cups flaked coconut
1 cup pecans, chopped
2 (9 inch) unbaked pie shells
Optional garnish for each slice:
      whipped cream and a maraschino cherry

Preheat oven to 350 degrees. Mix the sugar, cocoa and salt together. Add eggs and blend well. Stir in milk, vanilla, butter, coconut and nuts. Pour evenly into pie crusts and bake for 40 minutes.

Kentucky Race Day Pie

1/4 cup butter, softened
1 cup sugar
3 large eggs
3/4 cup light corn syrup
1 teaspoon vanilla
1 cup chocolate chips
1 cup chopped pecans
1/4 teaspoon salt
3 tablespoons bourbon
1 (9 inch) unbaked pie shell

Preheat oven to 350 degrees. Cream butter and sugar together. Add rest of the ingredients in order given, mixing well. Pour into pie shell and bake for 45 to 50 minutes.
When ready to serve, whip 1 cup heavy cream, add 1/4 cup powdered sugar and 1 tablespoon bourbon. Spread on top of pie or put a dollop on each serving. Sprinkle shaved chocolate and a few chopped pecans on top.

DOUBLE LAYER CHOCOLATE CHEESECAKE PIE

1 (9 inch) chocolate crumb pie crust
2 (8 ounce) packages cream cheese, softened
1/2 cup sugar
1/2 teaspoon vanilla
2 large eggs
3 (1 ounce each) squares semi-sweet chocolate, melted &
    slightly cooled

Preheat oven to 350 degrees. Beat cream cheese, sugar and vanilla with electric mixer on medium speed till fluffy. Add eggs, beating until well blended. Stir melted chocolate into *1 cup* of the batter. Pour this chocolate batter into crust; top with remaining plain batter. Bake in preheated oven for 40 minutes or until center is almost set. Cool. Refrigerate for 3 hours or overnight.

GRANDMA'S CHERRY CHEESE PIE

1 (9 inch) graham cracker pie crust
2 (8 ounce) packages cream cheese, softened
3/4 cup sugar
2 teaspoons lemon juice
1/2 teaspoon vanilla
3 large eggs
1 (21 ounce) can Cherry Pie Filling

Preheat oven to 325 degrees. Combine cream cheese, sugar, lemon juice and vanilla, beating well with mixer until lumps are gone. Add eggs, one at a time; pour into crust and bake for 30 minutes. Top with pie filling and chill. Serve with Cool Whip or sweetened whipped cream.

SWEETENED WHIPPED CREAM: Beat 1 cup whipping cream until soft peaks form. Fold in 2 tablespoons sifted powdered sugar and 1/2 teaspoon vanilla. Don't over beat or you'll have butter!

KEY LIME PIE

There are many versions. This is one of the best!

4 large eggs, separated
1 (14 ounce) can sweetened condensed milk
1/4 cup key lime juice
1 (9 inch) graham cracker pie crust

Beat the egg yolks with a whisk. Add the sweetened condensed milk. Slowly stir in the lime juice, beating, with whisk, until thickened. Pour into pie crust. Top with meringue.

MERINGUE:
4 egg whites
1/2 teaspoon cream of tartar
6 tablespoons sugar

Preheat oven to 350 degrees. Beat egg whites with cream of tartar until foamy. Slowly add sugar, one tablespoon at a time and beat at high speed till stiff but not dry. Spread on top of pie sealing to edges of crust. Bake for 15 minutes. Cool and refrigerate.

Pie Tip:

You can just spread frozen whipped topping, thawed, on top of pie instead of meringue but the meringue just tops it off. Besides, by using a meringue, you cook the eggs.
Nellie & Joe's Key West Lime Juice (the best one I've used) is in the specialty section or fruit juice section of your grocery store. The 16 ounce bottle will make *lots* of pies!

MILE HIGH LEMON PIE

Truly old fashioned and the best!

1 (9 inch) baked pie shell	5 large eggs, separated
1-1/2 cups sugar	2 tablespoons butter
1/3 cup cornstarch	2 teaspoons grated lemon peel
1/4 teaspoon salt	1/4 teaspoon cream of tartar
1-1/2 cups cold water	1/2 cup sugar
1/2 cup lemon juice	1/2 teaspoon vanilla

Preheat oven to 425 degrees. Bake pie shell for about 9 to 10 minutes and set aside. Combine the sugar, cornstarch and salt in a large saucepan. Over medium heat, gradually add water and lemon juice, stirring constantly with whisk till slightly thickened. Beat the egg yolks in a small bowl till lemon colored; whisk in some of the hot mixture, then whisk back into the saucepan. Cook over heat, stirring constantly until thick and bubbly. Cook one minute more and remove from heat. Stir in butter and lemon peel. Pour into baked pie shell.

MERINGUE:

Combine egg whites and cream of tartar. Beat until foamy. Gradually beat in the 1/2 cup sugar, beating till still peaks form. Beat in vanilla. With a large spoon, spoon over filling, sealing the edges. Shape large peaks with the back of the spoon. Sprinkle a little lemon rind on top. Bake at 350 degrees for 15 minutes. Chill before serving.

Pie Tip:

To "toast" pecans, spread them on a cookie sheet and place in a preheated 350 degree oven for 5 to 7 minutes, stirring often. Watch closely, they burn easily.

Fresh Peach Pie

1 cup sugar
1/4 cup cornstarch
1-1/2 cups water
4 tablespoons peach gelatin
1/2 teaspoon almond extract
4 cups fresh peaches, peeled & sliced
1 (9 inch) baked pie shell

Combine sugar, cornstarch and water in a medium saucepan. Bring to a boil and cook until thickened, stirring constantly. Remove from stove and dissolve gelatin in this hot syrup. Add almond extract and cool until lukewarm. Fold in peaches and spoon into pie shell. Chill in refrigerator for 3 hours. To serve, top with Cool Whip.

Note: *Choose tree-ripened fruit. Peaches don't sweeten once they're picked. Don't let looks deceive you. Peaches that look perfect, probably have had chemicals sprayed on them for cosmetic purposes. Mother Nature produces fruit like people, slightly imperfect! Don't squeeze peaches or you'll bruise them. Judge them by their color and stem end, which should be clear and yellow all around. Pass up hard green ones. Peaches are rich in vitamin A and have only about 50 calories per cup when eaten raw.*

Fresh Peach Crunch

Peel and slice **5 or 6 fresh peaches** in a pie plate; toss with a little **cinnamon/sugar.** Mix together, **1 cup packed light brown sugar and 3/4 cup flour;** cut in: **1/4 cup butter.** Cover peaches with this mixture and bake in 350 degree oven till peaches are fork tender and crumbs are brown and crispy. Serve with whipped cream.

DIANNE'S PECAN PIE

1 (9 inch) unbaked pie shell
1 cup pecans, chopped
3 large eggs, lightly beaten
Dash of salt

1 cup corn syrup
3/4 cup granulated sugar
1 teaspoon vanilla

Preheat oven to 350 degrees. Completely cover bottom of pie shell with the pecans. Combine the remaining ingredients and pour over pecans. The pecans will rise to the top in a couple of minutes. Bake for 45 to 50 minutes. Let cool at room temperature, it will firm up as it cools. Serve with a scoop of vanilla ice cream. Makes 6 to 8 servings

CHOCOLATE PECAN PIE:

1 (9 inch) unbaked pie shell
3/4 cup chocolate chips
3 large eggs, slightly beaten
2/3 cup sugar
1/2 cup light corn syrup

1/2 cup dark corn syrup
1/3 cup butter, melted
Dash of salt
1 cup pecan halves

Preheat oven to 350 degrees. Sprinkle chocolate chips on bottom of pie shell. Combine eggs, sugar, both corn syrups, butter and salt; beat well with a large spoon. Stir in pecans. Carefully pour over chocolate chips. *Cover edges* with foil. Bake for 25 minutes in preheated oven; *remove foil* and bake for 20 to 25 minutes. Refrigerate for 2 hours before serving.
Makes 6 to 8 servings

Turtle Cheesecake

In a medium saucepan combine:
1 (7 ounce) package caramel candies
1/4 cup evaporated milk
Stir constantly over low heat until caramels are melted and mixture is smooth.
Stir in:
1-1/2 cups pecans, chopped
Pour mixture into:
1 (9 inch) chocolate cookie pie crust
Combine the following in a food processor or blender and process until smooth:
6 ounces cream cheese, softened
1/2 cup sour cream
1-1/4 cups milk
Add:
1 (3.4 ounce) package instant chocolate pudding & pie filling
Drizzle over filling:
1/2 cup hot fudge topping
Sprinkle over fudge topping:
1-1/4 cups chopped pecans
Chill before serving.

Fresh Strawberry Pie

1 cup sugar
4 tablespoons cornstarch
4 tablespoons strawberry gelatin

1-1/2 cups water
4 cups fresh strawberries, sliced
1 (9 inch) baked pie shell

Combine sugar, cornstarch, gelatin and water in a saucepan and cook until thickened, stirring constantly. Cool till lukewarm. Fold in fresh strawberries. Spoon into pie shell and chill 3 hours before serving. Serve with Cool Whip & a fresh strawberry on top.

PINEAPPLE CHESS PIE

1-1/2 cups sugar
2 tablespoons cornmeal
4 large eggs
4 tablespoons butter melted
1/4 cup lemon juice
1 (8 ounce) can crushed pineapple, with juice

Milk
1 (9 inch) unbaked pie shell

Preheat oven to 425 degrees. Mix the sugar, cornmeal, eggs, butter and lemon juice together. Pour the pineapple, with juice and enough milk to make 3/4 cup. Add the above mixture. Stir to mix well. Pour into pie shell and bake for 10 minutes. Turn oven temperature down to 350° and bake for about 40 minutes more or until center is set and golden.

PINEAPPLE CRUNCH PIE

CRUST:
Mix together: **2 cups flour, 1/2 teaspoon salt, Cut in 1 cup butter and add 1 cup chopped pecans.** Press into 9x13x2 inch pan and bake at 350° for about 10 minutes, until light brown. Cool.

FILLING:
1 (8 ounce) package
   cream cheese, softened
1 cup powdered sugar
2 tablespoons milk
1 (8 ounce) carton Cool Whip

1 (20 ounce) can crushed
   pineapple, with juice
1-1/4 cups sugar
2 tablespoons cornstarch
Chopped pecans

Combine cream cheese, powdered sugar and milk. Spread over baked crust. Spread evenly with Cool Whip. In medium saucepan, combine pineapple, sugar and cornstarch and cook until thickened. Cool and gently spread over Cool Whip. Sprinkle top with chopped pecans.

PINEAPPLE CREAM PIE

2/3 cup sugar
4 tablespoons flour
1/4 teaspoon salt
3 large eggs, separated
1-1/2 cups milk
1 teaspoon vanilla
2 tablespoons butter
1-1/2 cups crushed pineapple, <u>well drained</u>
1 (9 inch) baked pie shell

Combine sugar, flour and salt in saucepan (not over heat yet). Mix well. Add egg yolks, stirring well and slowly add milk. Whisk until smooth. After adding all of the milk, _then_ place over medium heat and cook, stirring constantly until thickened, about 5 minutes. Remove from heat and add vanilla, butter and crushed pineapple. Pour into baked pie shell. Add the meringue (below) and proceed.

MERINGUE: 3 egg whites, 1/4 teaspoon cream of tartar, 6 tablespoons sugar and 1 teaspoon vanilla. Beat egg whites with cream of tartar until foamy. Slowly add sugar, 1 tablespoon at a time, beating until stiff. Add vanilla. Bake at 350 degrees for 15 minutes.

NOTE: This is an easier way to do a cream filling and it works. This is also good for banana pudding, by adding 3 sliced bananas. Line a 2 quart casserole with vanilla wafers, a layer of bananas & repeat. Add the meringue and bake the meringue as directed.

Pie Tip:

For the best lemon flavor in any lemon dessert, always use a fresh lemon for the juice and peel. And use only the bright yellow zest and not the biter white pith.

SWEET POTATO PIE

A southern staple and Grandpa Emery's favorite!

1 (9 inch) unbaked pie shell
1 large egg white
1-1/2 cups canned sweet potatoes
2/3 cup sugar
2 tablespoons butter, melted
2 tablespoons lemon juice

1/2 teaspoon nutmeg
1/2 teaspoon mace
1/2 teaspoon vanilla
1/2 teaspoon salt
3 large eggs, beaten
1 cup half & half

Preheat oven to 450 degrees. Prick pie shell on bottom and sides with a fork. Bake for 9 to 10 minutes. Brush the beaten egg white on bottom of pie shell and set aside to cool. Reduce oven temperature to 350 degrees. In mixer bowl, beat sweet potatoes and sugar till very smooth. Add butter, lemon juice, nutmeg, mace, vanilla and salt. Beat well. Add eggs and half & half. Beat till smooth. Pour into pie shell and bake about 60 minutes till center tests done with a tooth pick. Serve with whipped cream.

CREAMY PUMPKIN PIE

1-3/4 cups solid pack pumpkin
1 (14 ounce) can sweetened
       condensed milk
1 large egg
1/2 teaspoon salt

1/2 teaspoon cinnamon
1/4 teaspoon nutmeg
1/4 teaspoon ginger
1 cup hot water
1 (9 inch) unbaked pie shell

Preheat oven to 375 degrees. Beat all ingredients together with electric mixer; pour mixture into pie shell and bake for 50 to 55 minutes till knife inserted in middle comes out clean.

VINEGAR PIE

Granny's old fashioned favorite

6 large eggs
2 cups sugar
1/2 cup butter, melted

1 tablespoon apple cider vinegar
1 teaspoon vanilla
1 (9 inch) unbaked pie shell

Preheat oven to 350 degrees. Mix all ingredients together by hand. Pour into pie shell and bake for 45 to 50 minutes till center is set. *Scrumptious!*

QUICK PUMPKIN PIE

1 (15 ounce) can solid pack pumpkin (1-3/4 cups)
1 (14 ounce) sweetened condensed milk
2 large eggs
1 teaspoon cinnamon
1/2 teaspoon each ginger and nutmeg
1/2 teaspoon salt
1 (9 inch) unbaked pie shell

Preheat oven to 425 degrees. Beat all of the ingredients together until smooth. Pour into pie crust and bake at 425 degrees for 15 minutes.
Reduce heat to 350 degrees and bake 35 to 40 minutes more until center tests done.
Chill before serving.
Makes 8 servings.
Serve with Cool Whip.

Kelley
1997

PUMPKIN PIE

My <u>favorite</u> pumpkin pie is the one I make with Libby's Pumpkin Pie Mix. The results are a great tasting, beautifully finished pie. And by using the Pillsbury All-Ready Pie Crust, it looks homemade! Because you are so busy preparing the other food for your holiday dinner, several of these pies would make your work easier. But, if you wish to mix your own, here is a good recipe:

1 (16 ounce) solid pack pumpkin (2 cups)
3/4 cup sugar
1 teaspoon cinnamon
1/2 teaspoon ginger
1/2 teaspoon nutmeg
1/2 teaspoon salt
3 large eggs, lightly beaten
2/3 cup (5-1/3 ounce can) evaporated milk
1/2 cup sweet milk
1 (9 inch) unbaked pie shell

Preheat oven to 375 degrees. Mix the first 6 ingredients together with an electric mixer, beating till smooth. Add eggs and milk, beat well and pour into pie shell. Bake for 25 to 30 minutes. Test center with a toothpick. If edges brown too quickly, cover with strips of aluminum foil.
Cool on wire rack before cutting.
Serve with whipped cream or whipped topping.

Raggedy Ann was as big as
Hannah.
Christmas 1983

TRIPPLE LAYER PUMPKIN PIE

A dessert lover's gourmet feast!

FIRST LAYER:
Beat till smooth:
1 (8 ounce) package cream cheese, softened
Add and beat till light & fluffy:
1//4 cup sugar
1/2 teaspoon vanilla
1 large egg, beaten
Chill for 30 minutes.
Spread into:
1 (9 inch) unbaked pie shell

SECOND LAYER:
Preheat oven to 350 degrees. Mix the following together, beating until thoroughly combined:

1-1/4 cups pumpkin puree	**1/4 cup white sugar**
1 cup evaporated milk	**1 teaspoon cinnamon**
2 large eggs, beaten	**1/4 teaspoon nutmeg**
1/4 cup light brown sugar, packed	**1/4 teaspoon salt**

Pour this mixture over the first (cream cheese) layer. Cover the edges with foil and bake in preheated oven for 25 minutes. *Remove* foil and bake 25 minutes *more.*

THIRD LAYER:
While pie is baking, mix 3rd layer.
Combine: **2 tablespoons all-purpose flour**
  2 tablespoons light brown sugar, packed
  Add: **2 tablespoons melted butter**
Stir until well combined and then <u>add</u>: **1/2 cup chopped pecans**
Sprinkle this 3rd layer over hot pie and bake fore 10 to 15 minutes more until toothpick comes out clean when inserted in center.   Makes 8 servings

2 LAYER PUMPKIN PIE

FIRST LAYER:
4 ounces cream cheese, softened (cut 8 ounce package in half)
1 tablespoon milk
1 tablespoon sugar
1-1/2 cups Cool Whip

Beat the softened cream cheese, milk and sugar together.
Gently stir in Cool Whip. Spread on bottom of:
1 (9 inch) graham cracker pie crust.

SECOND LAYER:
1 cup cold milk
2 (3.4 ounce) packages instant vanilla pie & pudding filling
1 (16 ounce) can solid pack pumpkin
1 teaspoon cinnamon
1/2 teaspoon ginger
1/4 teaspoon nutmeg

Beat with a wire whisk until well blended. Carefully spread over the
first (cream cheese) layer.
Chill at least 4 hours or until
set. Makes 8 servings   Top
each serving with Cool Whip

Megan holding Natalie.
They're great friends as
well as first cousins.
1999

GRANNY'S IRRESISTIBLE DESSERTS & COOKIES

RECIPES:

DESSERTS:

COOKIES:

IRISH COFFEE MOUSSE

1 (3.4 ounce) package instant vanilla pudding & pie filling
2 tablespoons instant coffee powder
3-1/2 cups milk
3 generous tablespoons Irish Whiskey
1/3 cup water
1 envelope Dream Whip topping mix
Garnishes: whipped cream & chocolate shavings

Combine pudding mix, coffee powder and milk; beat just until blended. Add whiskey and water; beat for 2 minutes. Prepare Dream Whip as directed on package, whipping until soft peaks form. Fold into creamed pudding mixture. Place in individual serving dishes. Chill; when ready to serve top with whipped cream and shaved Hershey's chocolate bar. Makes 6 servings

APRICOT RITZ
A very nice dessert for a game dinner

4 (17 ounce) cans apricot halves
1 (4 ounce) stack of Ritz crackers
2/3 cup light brown sugar, firmly packed
1/4 cup butter, melted

Preheat oven to 300 degrees. Crush the crackers to make crumbs. In a 2 quart casserole dish, alternate layers (*in order given*) of apricots, crumbs and brown sugar. Pour melted butter evenly over top. Bake for about 45 minutes. So easy!
Makes 6 servings

ANGEL DESSERT SQUARES

A 1928 dessert. I made it a lot in 1963 for wedding and baby showers. A great ladies' party dessert.

1 cup finely crushed vanilla wafer crumbs
3/4 cup butter, softened
2 cups sifted powdered sugar
2 large egg yolks
2 large egg whites, stiffly beaten
1 (15.25 ounce) can crushed pineapple, well drained
1/2 cup pecans, chopped

Spread *1/2* of the crumbs on bottom of a well buttered 8 x 8 x 2 inch dish. Cream butter, gradually adding powdered sugar; beat until light and fluffy. Add egg yolks, one at a time, beating well after each addition. Fold in beaten egg whites. Beat a medium speed a few seconds or until smooth. Fold in pineapple and nuts. Carefully spread this mixture over crumbs. Top with *remaining* crumbs. Chill until firm, 6 hours or overnight. To serve cut into 6 squares and garnish with maraschino cherries. This recipe can be doubled and put in a 9 x 13 inch dish.

PINEAPPLE AU GRATIN

2 (20 ounce) cans pineapple chunks, drained, reserve juice
1 cup sugar
6 tablespoons flour
2 cups sharp Cheddar cheese, grated
1/2 cup melted margarine
1 cup Ritz crackers, crushed

Preheat oven to 350 degrees. Combine sugar, flour and pineapple juice. Add cheese and pineapple, mixing well. Pour into a 9 x 13 baking pan. Combine margarine and cracker crumbs and sprinkle over top. Bake for 25 to 30 minutes. Makes 12 to 15 servings.

Shirley Smith

STRAWBERRY CRUNCH

Step 1:
1 cup all-purpose flour   1/2 cup margarine
1/4 cup light brown sugar   1/2 cup chopped nuts

Preheat oven to 250 degrees. Blend like pie dough. Put into 9x13x2 pan and bake for 1 hour, *stirring* 2 or 3 times during baking to brown evenly.

Step 2:
2 large egg whites   1 cup white sugar
1 tablespoon lemon juice   1 teaspoon vanilla
1 pint frozen strawberries,
      with juice

In a large mixing bowl, break berries apart with a fork. Add rest of ingredients and beat with mixer beater 20 minutes.

Step 3:
1 pint whipping cream
Whip the whipping cream and fold into the #2 mixture.
Use *1/2* of the crumbs in the bottom of a 9 x 13 inch dish.
Cover with the strawberry mixture, top with the remaining crumbs. Freeze overnight.
Makes 12 servings

Grandma & Grandpa
at Myrtle Beach, SC
Sept. 2000

Strawberry Pretzel Dessert

CRUST:
2 cups coarsely crushed pretzels
3/4 cup butter or margarine, melted
3 tablespoons sugar
Mix together & press firmly into bottom of a 9x13 baking pan.
Bake at 375 degrees about 8 minutes. Cool

FILLING:
1 (8 ounce) package cream cheese, softened
1 cup sugar
1 (8 ounce) carton Cool Whip
Beat cream cheese & sugar together. Fold in Cool Whip. Spread
over cooled crust and refrigerate 10 to 15 minutes.

TOPPING:
1 (6 ounce) package. strawberry gelatin
2 cups boiling water
Dissolve gelatin in boiling water. Let this congeal to the consistency of egg whites, about 15 minutes.
Then stir in:
2 (10 ounce) packages frozen strawberries, thawed.
Pour over cheese layer and chill till firm.
Makes 12 servings

MAKE YOUR OWN SWEETENED CONDENSED MILK

1 cup nonfat instant dry milk powder
2/3 cup sugar
1/3 cup boiling water
3 tablespoons butter, melted

Put all of this in a blender. Process till smooth, then refrigerate.
It makes 1 cup. It sets up quick and really works! Will keep in the
fridge several weeks. Can be doubled.

FOUR LAYER DESSERT

Mary Jane Howard's Plantation recipe

FIRST LAYER:
Combine:
1-1/2 cups all-purpose flour
3/4 cup melted butter
1 cup pecans
Mix well. Pat into 9x13 inch baking pan. Bake at 325 degrees for 20 minutes. Cool

SECOND LAYER:
Beat together until smooth:
12 ounces cream cheese, softened
1-1/2 cups powdered sugar
1 (8 ounce) container Cool Whip
Spread over baked layer.

THIRD LAYER:
2 (3.4 ounce) packages chocolate instant pudding & pie filling
3 cups milk
Mix together and pour over 2nd layer.

FOURTH LAYER:
Top with 8 ounces of Cool Whip
Sprinkle with 1/2 cup chopped pecans.
Chill, covered for 24 hours before serving.

My parents,
Ralph & Shirley
Cooper
1944

SOUR CREAM APPLE SQUARES

This is the recipe for the apple squares we sold in our Home Sweet Home Bakery in 1984

2 cups all-purpose flour
2 cups brown sugar, packed
1/2 cup butter, softened
1 cup chopped nuts
2 teaspoons cinnamon
2 cups finely chopped peeled
      apples

1/2 teaspoon salt
1 teaspoon baking soda
1 cup sour cream
1 teaspoon vanilla
1 large egg

Preheat oven to 350 degrees. Measure and sift flour. In a large bowl, combine flour, sugar and butter until crumbly. Stir in nuts. Press _2-3/4 cups_ of the crumb mixture into <u>ungreased</u> 9x13 inch baking pan. To the *remaining* crumb mixture, add cinnamon, salt, baking soda, sour cream, vanilla, and egg, mixing well. Stir in apples; spoon evenly over base. Bake for 35 to 40 minutes or until toothpick inserted in center comes out clean.
Cut into squares. Serve with Cool Whip or ice cream.
Makes 12 servings.

DECADENT AMBROSIA DESSERT

1 (11 ounce) can Mandarin oranges, drained
1 (8 ounce) can crushed pineapple, drained
1 (7 ounce) can shredded coconut
2 cups miniature marshmallows
1/2 cup milk
3-1/2 cups Cool Whip

Combine the oranges, pineapple, coconut and marshmallows together in a large bowl. Lightly stir the milk and Cool Whip together and fold into fruit mixture. Chill at least 1 hour. Makes 12 servings

Fresh Blueberry Brulee

1 (8 ounce) package cream cheese
6 tablespoons sugar
1-1/2 cups sour cream
1 teaspoon vanilla

2 pints blueberries
Light brown sugar

With electric beaters, beat cream cheese until light and fluffy. Add sugar and beat 1 minute more; add sour cream and vanilla, beating on low speed till blended. Arrange blueberries in bottom of a 9 inch oven-proof baking dish. Spread cream cheese mixture evenly over top and sprinkle with brown sugar. Place under broiler, about 4 or 5 inches from heat, for about 2 minutes until sugar melts and caramelizes. Serve warm (not hot). Makes 9 servings.

Pineapple Casserole

A great side dish for game or ham.

1/2 cup butter
1 cup sugar
4 large eggs

1/8 teaspoon nutmeg
5 pieces bread, torn into pieces
1 (20 ounce) can crushed pineapple,
        with juice

Preheat oven to 350 degrees. Cream butter and sugar until light and fluffy. Add eggs, one at a time, beating well after each addition. Add cinnamon and nutmeg, beating for 1/2 minute more. Carefully stir in bread pieces and pineapple. Spread evenly in a greased 9 x 9 inch baking dish. Bake for 1 hour. Makes 9 servings.

Granny Says:

I quit jogging for health reasons.
My thighs rubbed together so much,
they caught my underwear on fire!!

PINEAPPLE AU GRATIN #2

2 cups self-rising flour
2 cups sugar
3 (20 ounce) cans pineapple chunks,
        reserving 1-1/2 cups of the juice
1 cup sharp Cheddar cheese, shredded
1/2 cup butter, melted
2 rolls Ritz crackers, crushed

Preheat oven to 350 degrees. Combine flour and sugar. Stir the
1-1/2 cups of reserved pineapple juice into flour/sugar mixture;
add pineapple and cheese. Pour into a buttered 9 x 13 inch baking
dish. Cover top with foil and bake for 30 minutes. Uncover and
stir; bake 10 minutes longer. Combine melted butter and cracker
crumbs; sprinkle over pineapple mixture. Return to oven for 10 to
15 minutes or until a knife inserted in center come out clean.
Makes 16 to 20 servings
NOTE: This popular recipe is from the "Back Home" restaurant in
Elizabethtown, Kentucky. Their recipe calls for 70 butter-flavored
crackers, crushed which is about 2 rolls of Ritz crackers.

GRAM'S BREAD PUDDING

1 cup fresh bread crumbs   1/2 cup sugar
2 cups milk, scalded   2 large eggs, beaten
1/4 teaspoon cinnamon   1/2 teaspoon vanilla
2 tablespoons melted butter   Dash of salt

Preheat oven to 350 degrees. Mix all together and pour into a
greased 8 x 8 x 2 inch baking dish. Bake for 30 minutes.
Serve with homemade vanilla ice cream or real whipped cream.
Makes 9 servings.

MISS DEE'S BREAD PUDDING With "Tipsy" Sauce

This was such a favorite in my little "Home Sweet Home Bakery. Customers would ooh and ahh and say it reminded them of their grandmother's kitchen. We made it fresh every day from our homemade cinnamon rolls that were left over from the day before. That was our secret! Now I save all left-over rolls, biscuits, whatever. I put them in my food processor, bag them and keep them in my freezer for instant bread pudding. Bread pudding is good for breakfast, a snack or dessert. You could even buy day-old cinnamon rolls from the bakery thrift store. They make such good bread pudding because they're already sweet with cinnamon and sugar. It doesn't matter that they have icing on top, all the better! Economical and wonderful!

1 pound of left-over bread, donuts, biscuits, etc.
   pulsed into very coarse crumbs...one pound is
   about 8 cups. (you don't have to be too exact)
1/2 cup sugar
1/2 teaspoon nutmeg
3 large eggs
1/4 cup butter, melted
1 (12 ounce) can evaporated milk
1 cup dark raisins

Mix *everything* together well and pour into a butter 9 inch square pan or 7-1/2 x 11-3/4 inch pan. Bake at 350° for 30 to 35 minutes. Pour the following sauce over top while it's still warm.

SAUCE:
Combine in a small saucepan:

1 tablespoons butter	**3 tablespoons water**
3/4 cup sugar	

Bring to a boil and boil for 3 minutes, stirring constantly (be sure and time it). Remove from heat and add **3 tablespoons bourbon (or lemon juice)**. Pour over warm bread pudding and brush on evenly. This recipe doubled is baked in a 9x13x2 inch baking dish and cut into 12 squares. This is not soupy but nice and moist.

FRESH APPLE COBBLER

FILLING:
5 cups (about 5-1/2 cups) cooking apples, peeled & sliced
3/4 cup sugar
2 tablespoons flour
1 tablespoon lemon juice
1 teaspoon vanilla
1/2 teaspoon cinnamon
1/4 teaspoon salt
1/4 cup water
2 tablespoons butter

Combine first 8 ingredients together and place in 9x13x2 inch butter baking dish. Dot with butter

BATTER:
1/2 cup flour
1/2 cup sugar
1/2 teaspoon salt
1/2 teaspoon baking powder
2 tablespoons butter, softened
1 large egg, lightly beaten

Preheat oven at 375 degrees. In medium bowl, combine all ingredients, beating with spoon till smooth. Drop by big dollops over filling, spacing evenly. Batter will spread during baking. Bake at in preheated oven for 35 to 45 minutes till apples are tender and crust is golden. Serve warm with heavy cream or whipped cream.

Granny Says:
Don't smooth cobbler toppings.
They should resemble "cobble" stones.

GRANDMA NITZ'S GERMAN APPLE TORTE

1 large egg	1/2 teaspoon salt
3/4 cup sugar	1 cup apples, peeled & diced
1/2 cup all-purpose flour	1/2 cup walnuts, chopped
1 teaspoon baking powder	1 teaspoon vanilla

Preheat oven to 350 degrees. Beat egg with electric mixer until light and lemon colored; gradually beat in sugar, beating till thick and pale in color. Sift the flour, baking powder and salt together; gently folding into egg mixture. Add apples, walnuts and vanilla, stirring until well mixed. Spread batter in an 8 inch round or square baking dish. Bake for 35 to 40 minutes until top is brown and crunchy. Serve warm with whipped cream or vanilla ice cream. Makes 6 servings

GRANDMA DEE'S APPLE CRISP

9 large cooking apples
1/2 cup sugar
1 cup all-purpose flour
1 cup light brown sugar, firmly packed
1 teaspoon baking powder
1/2 teaspoon salt
1 large egg, beaten
1/2 cup (1 stick) butter, melted

Preheat oven to 350 degrees. Peel and slice apples thin. Toss them with 1/2 cup sugar and place in a 9 x 13 inch baking dish. In a small bowl make a mixture of the flour, brown sugar, baking powder and salt. Stir in the beaten egg. It will be messy but carefully, as evenly as you can, spread this mixture over the apples. Drizzle the melted butter evenly over top. Bake uncovered, for 1 hour. Leaving it uncovered gives it a golden brown, crispy, crunchy top.

APPLE BROWN BETTY

5 tablespoons butter, melted
2 cups fresh bread crumbs
1/2 cup light or dark brown sugar, firmly packed
5 cups cooking apples, peeled and sliced
1/2 teaspoon cinnamon
1/2 tablespoon lemon juice
1/3 cup hot water

Preheat oven to 350 degrees. Butter a 1-1/2 quart baking dish.
Toss butter and bread crumbs together. Spread about *1/3* of the
crumbs in the baking dish. Toss the apples with the cinnamon
and lemon juice. Spread 1/2 of the apple mixture over the crumbs.
Repeat (the other half of apple mixture, 1/3 of the crumbs). End
with the last 1/3 of the crumbs on top. Sprinkle the hot water
over the top. Bake, covered, at for 25 minutes. *Uncover* and
bake another 20 minutes more. Serve with whipped cream.
Makes 6 to 8 servings

PEACH-COCONUT CRISP

1 (29 ounce) can sliced peaches, with juice
1 (18.25 ounce) package yellow cake mix
1/2 cup butter, melted
1 cup flaked coconut
1 cup pecans, chopped

Preheat oven to 325 degrees. Put all of the above in an
ungreased 9 x 13 inch baking dish in the order given. Bake
for 1 hour. Serve with Cool Whip or vanilla ice cream.
Makes 8 servings

Rhubarb-Strawberry Crunch

3 cups rhubarb, diced
1 cup fresh strawberries, sliced

1 cup granulated sugar
3 tablespoons flour

Mix all four of the above together in a large bowl, coating fruit well. Spray a 9 x 13 inch baking dish with Pam and place mixture evenly on bottom. Add topping.

TOPPING:
1-1/2 cups all-purpose flour
1 cup light brown sugar,
    firmly packed

1 cup rolled oats
1 cup cold butter

Preheat oven to 375 degrees. Mix flour, sugar and oats together. Cut in butter to resemble crumbs. Sprinkle over fruit mixture. Bake for 45 minutes. Serve with vanilla ice cream.
Makes 8 servings.

Easy No-Cook Banana Pudding

2 (3.4 oz.) packages vanilla instant pudding filling
3 cups milk
1 (14 ounce) can sweetened condensed milk
2 (8 ounce) cartons Cool Whip
1 (12 ounce) box vanilla wafers
5 or 6 bananas, sliced

Whisk together the pudding mix and milk in a large bowl until thickened. Whisk in the sweetened condensed milk. Fold in **one** of the 8 oz. cartons of Cool Whip and mix well. In the bottom of a 9 x 13 inch dish, layer half of the vanilla wafers, sliced bananas and pudding mixture. Repeat layers. Top with 2nd carton of Cool Whip. Sprinkle a few cookie crumbs on top. Chill, covered, over-night. Makes 12 servings

PINEAPPLE CRISP

CRUST:

1-1/2 cups flaked coconut

1 cup all-purpose flour

1/8 teaspoon salt

1 cup light brown sugar

1/2 cup butter, melted

Combine coconut, flour, salt, and brown sugar. Mix in butter. Press *1-1/2 cups* of this mixture into a greased 9 x 9 inch baking dish. Set aside the *remaining* mixture.

FILLING:

3/4 cup sugar

3 tablespoons cornstarch

1 (8 ounce) can crushed pineapple,
        undrained

1 tablespoon lemon juice

1 tablespoon butter

Preheat oven to 350 degrees. Combine all of the filling ingredients together in a medium saucepan. Bring to a boil and cook, stirring constantly for 2 minutes or until thickened. Spread filling over crust. Spread the *reserved* crust mixture over top. Bake for 25 to 30 minutes. Makes 9 servings.

ESCALLOPED APPLES

6 medium apples

1/2 teaspoon cinnamon

1/4 teaspoon salt

1 teaspoon lemon juice

1/4 cup water

3/4 cup brown sugar, packed

1/4 cup flour

1/3 cup butter

Preheat oven to 400 degrees. Peel, core and slice apples in 1/2 inch pieces; place in buttered 9 x 13 baking dish. Add cinnamon, salt, lemon juice and water. Mix the brown sugar, flour and butter together until crumbly and sprinkle evenly over top. Bake, uncovered, in preheated oven for 30 minutes or until apples are fork-tender. Makes 8 servings

Old Fashioned Banana Pudding

Grandpa Emery's favorite dessert!

1/4 cup sugar	1 tablespoon butter
3-1/2 tablespoons cornstarch	1 teaspoon vanilla
1/2 teaspoon salt	1 teaspoon banana extract
2-1/2 cups milk	3 or 4 bananas, sliced
3 large egg yolks	Vanilla Wafers
1/4 cup sugar	Meringue (below)

Combine 1/4 cup sugar, cornstarch and salt in top of a double boiler. Add the milk gradually, stirring constantly. Cook over boiling water until thickened, stirring constantly. Beat the egg yolks and 1/4 cup sugar together with a fork, in a small bowl until pale yellow. Add a little of the hot mixture, then pour back in with the rest of the hot mixture. Cook about 2 minutes, stirring. Remove from heat and add butter, vanilla and banana extract. Line a 2 quart baking dish with vanilla wafers, bottom & sides. Pour *1/3* of the custard over the wafers, add *1/2* of the sliced bananas. Repeat layers ending on top with a layer of custard. Cover with the meringue (below) Makes 8 servings.
Refrigerate between servings.

MERINGUE:

Preheat oven to 350 degrees. Beat **3 egg whites** till foamy. Slowly add **6 tablespoons sugar,** 2 tablespoons at a time, beating well after each addition. Spoon this over top of custard. Place in preheated oven and bake for 15 minutes till meringue is light brown. Watch, do not let it burn.

Pie Tip:

Adding the sugar _slowly_ to the egg whites, dissolves the sugar and helps to keep the finished pie from "beading" later.

GINGERBREAD WITH LEMON SAUCE
Great old fashioned cake

3/4 cup dark brown sugar
3/4 cup dark molasses
3/4 cup shortening, melted
2 large eggs, slightly beaten
2-1/2 cups all-purpose flour
1/2 teaspoon baking powder

2 teaspoons ginger
1-1/2 teaspoons cinnamon
1/2 teaspoon cloves
1/2 teaspoon nutmeg
1 cup boiling water

Preheat oven to 350 degrees. Mix sugar, molasses and shortening together. Add eggs and mix well. Sift dry ingredients together and beat until well blended. Add to the sugar mixture. Then add boiling water and beat on low speed until smooth. The batter will be very thin. Pour into a greased and floured 9 x 13 inch baking dish. Bake for 30 to 40 minutes. While still hot, pour lemon sauce (below) over top. Makes 15 servings.

LEMON SAUCE

3/4 cup white sugar
2 tablespoons cornstarch
2 cups water
Grated rind of 2 lemons

Dash of salt
1/4 cup butter
1/4 cup lemon juice

Mix the sugar and cornstarch together. Add water and cook until thick and clear. Remove from heat and stir in remaining ingredients. Pour over hot gingerbread.

BOUDACIOUS FRUIT COBBLER

1 cup self-rising flour
1 cup sugar
1/2 cup butter

1 cup milk
2 cups fruit or berries, your choice

Preheat oven to 350 degrees. Melt butter in 2 quart baking dish. Mix flour, sugar and milk together and pour over melted butter. Carefully pour in fruit; DO NOT STIR. Bake 55 minutes.   Makes: 8 servings.

Tiramisu

6 large egg yolks
1-1/4 cups sugar
1-1/4 cups mascarpone cheese
1-3/4 cups whipping cream
2 tablespoons instant coffee crystals
3/4 cup water
2 tablespoons Kahlua

2 (3 ounces each) packages ladyfingers
2 ounces semi-sweet chocolate, grated

Combine the egg yolks and sugar, beating until thick and lemon colored, about 1 minute. Place in top of a double boiler and cook on simmering water for 8 to 10 minutes, stirring constantly. Remove from heat and add mascarpone cheese, beating well. Whip the whipping cream until stiff peaks form and fold into egg mixture. Dissolve instant coffee crystals in 3/4 cup water and add Kahlua. Line a 9 inch square dish with ladyfingers, flat side up. Brush with coffee mixture. Spoon half of the egg yolk/cheese mixture. Sprinkle with grated chocolate. Repeat with another layer of ladyfingers, brush with coffee mixture; spoon rest of cheese mixture on top of that. Sprinkle with grated chocolate. Cover tightly with foil and chill 8 hours or overnight. To serve, cut into 3 inch squares, sprinkle with powdered sugar and top with a maraschino cherry.   Makes 9 servings.
This is rich, you may want to cut smaller servings.

NOTE: Mascarpone cheese is a soft Italian sweet cheese, very much like cream cheese. It's in the dairy section or gourmet cheese section of the super market. It comes in an 8 ounce flat-looking tube. One tub is 8 ounces so you will need to buy 2 tubs and measure out 1-1/4 cups. Freeze the un-used portion for your next Tiramisu.

CRÈME BRULEE

It's just Granny's fancy pudding.

3/4 cup sugar	3 cups whipping cream
6 large egg yolks	1/2 cup milk
1 tablespoon vanilla	Brown sugar

Mix sugar with egg yolks and vanilla, beating with a wire whisk just until combined. Scald whipping cream and milk (bring just to the boiling point, do not let boil). Slowly add the milk mixture to the egg mixture, stirring constantly. Pour into 8 small oven-proof custard dishes. Place in a pan with water half-way up sides of custard dishes. Preheat oven to 350 degrees and bake for 30 minutes till set. Cool. Just before serving, sprinkle some brown sugar on top of each custard and place under the broiler to caramelize. You want a nice "crust" on top. Serve at room temperature. Makes 8 servings.

Serve with instant cappuccino coffee and your best homemade cookies!

MOTHER'S BAKED APPLES

6 large baking apples,	2 teaspoons nutmeg
6 tablespoons brown sugar	3 tablespoons butter
2 teaspoons cinnamon	1 cup apple cider

Preheat oven to 350 degrees. Slice about 1 inch off the top of each apple and core center almost to the bottom. Do not peel. Place a tablespoon brown sugar into the hole of each apple and sprinkle each one with a little cinnamon and nutmeg. Top with 1/2 tablespoon butter. Replace top. Place apples in a 9 x 13 baking dish and pour apple cider over each one. Bake in preheated oven uncovered about 1 hour or until apples are tender; basting often with the cider. To serve, pour a little cream over the top of each one. Makes 6 servings.

Nanaimo bars

This is the original 1950's recipe from the city of Nanaimo, Vancouver Island, British Columbia.

FIRST LAYER:

1/2 cup butter
1/4 cup sugar
5 tablespoons unsweetened cocoa
Combine these 3 ingredients in top of double boiler over barely simmering water. Stir occasionally till melted.
ADD: **1 large egg, beaten**
Stir to cook and thicken. Remove from heat and stir in:
1-1/4 cups graham cracker crumbs
1 cup flaked coconut
1/2 cup finely chopped almonds
Press into ungreased 8 x 8 x 2 inch dish.

SECOND LAYER:

1/2 cup butter
2 tablespoons + 2 teaspoons cream
2 tablespoons vanilla pudding powder
Cream these together and gradually beat in:
2 cups powdered sugar
Beat until light & fluffy and spread over bottom layer. Chill

THIRD LAYER:

4 squares semi-sweet chocolate
2 tablespoons unsalted butter
Melt these 2 together over low heat. Cool. While cool but still liquid, pour over 2nd layer. Chill in fridge.
Cut into bars. Makes 16 to 24 cookies.

NOTE: This recipe was also the prize winner in the Toronto Sun newspaper. The only difference, the winner used 1-3/4 cup graham cracker crumbs in the first layer. Since the 1950's there has been an on-going debate in Canada as to the origin of the recipe.

FUDGE BROWNIES
Super easy and good.

1/2 cup butter	2 large eggs
6 tablespoons Hershey's cocoa	1 teaspoon vanilla
2 tablespoons shortening	2/3 cup all-purpose flour
1 cup granulated sugar	1 cup nuts, chopped

Preheat oven to 350 degrees. In a medium saucepan, melt butter, cocoa and shortening over low heat; stir in sugar, eggs and vanilla. Using a wooden spoon, beat lightly by hand just until combined. Stir in flour and pecans or walnuts. Spread in a greased 9 x 9 inch baking dish. Bake for 20 minutes. Cool on wire cake rack before cutting into squares. If using an 8 inch square pan, bake for 25 minutes.

BROWNIES A LA MODE: Cut brownies into 4 large squares and top with vanilla ice cream. If you don't count calories, top each serving with a little Hershey's chocolate syrup and sprinkle with chopped nuts.

OPTIONAL CHOCOLATE GLAZE:
In a saucepan, cook and stir:
3 tablespoons butter or margarine, 2 tablespoons cocoa powder and 2 tablespoons milk until mixture comes to a boil.
Remove from heat. Stir in: **1-1/2 cups sifted powdered sugar and 1/2 teaspoon vanilla** until smooth.
Spread over cooled brownies.

CREAM CHEESE BROWNIES

FIRST STEP:
Cream together:
1 (8 ounce) cream cheese, softened
4 tablespoons (1/4 cup) butter
Add and cream until fluffy:
1/2 cup sugar
Then blend in:
2 large eggs
2 tablespoons flour
1 teaspoon vanilla

SECOND STEP:
Melt over low heat, stirring constantly:
2 (4 ounce) packages German Sweet Chocolate
6 tablespoons butter
Cool.

THIRD STEP:
Beat until light: **4 large eggs;** add: **1-/2 cups sugar; sift to-gether: 1-1/2 cups all-purpose flour, 1 teaspoon baking powder, 1/2 teaspoon salt and blend into the chocolate mixture.**
Add: **2 teaspoons vanilla and 1/2 teaspoon almond extract**

Preheat oven to 350 degrees. Spread *1/2* of the chocolate mixture into a greased 9 x 13 inch baking pan. Spread *all* of the cream cheese mixture over that. Then, in *big spoonfuls,* drop the rest of the chocolate mixture over cream cheese mixture. with a knife, swirl through only the top two layers. Bake for 35 minutes. Cool and cut into squares or bars. For 32 squares, cut 6 across and 8 down. For 16 bars, cut 6 across and 4 down.

FOR ICING: Whisk together 2 cups sifted powdered sugar, 1 teaspoon vanilla and a few drops of milk. It should be thick. From the end of the whisk, drizzle across brownies before cutting them.

MOTHER'S BROWNIES

Melt together & cool:
1 stick butter
2 (1 ounce each) squares semi-sweet chocolate
Add and beat well:

2 large eggs	**1 cup sugar**
3/4 cup all-purpose flour	**1 teaspoon vanilla**

Stir in:
1 cup chopped pecans
Preheat oven to 325 degrees. Pour into 9x13 inch baking pan and bake for 20 to 25 minutes. Then add glaze.
GLAZE:
1 cup confectioners' sugar
Add enough Hershey's chocolate syrup to spread

MOM'S CHOCOLATE CHIP COOKIES

Sift together & set aside:
2-1/4 cups all-purpose flour
1 teaspoon baking soda
1/2 teaspoon salt
Beat together:
1 cup butter
3/4 cup light brown sugar, packed
3/4 cup granulated sugar
1 teaspoon vanilla
2 large eggs
Blend in flour mixture.
Stir in:
1 cup chopped nuts
1 (12 ounce) package chocolate chips
Drop by teaspoonfuls, 2 inches apart, on <u>un</u>greased cookie sheets. Bake at 375 degrees for 10 to 12 minutes. Makes 6 doz.

GRANDMA "G"s BROWN SUGAR COOKIES   Agnes Gerock

1 cup butter
1 pound box light brown sugar
2 large eggs, slightly beaten
2-1/2 cups all-purpose flour

1/4 teaspoon salt
1/4 teaspoon baking soda
1 cup chopped pecans

Preheat oven to 350 degrees. Cream butter and sugar; add eggs. Sift flour, salt and baking soda together and add to creamed mixture. Mix well. Add pecans. Drop by teaspoonfuls on greased baking sheet. Bake in preheated oven for about 20 minutes. Makes about 2 dozen cookies

GRANDMA "G"s SHORTIES   Agnes Gerock

1 cup (2 sticks) margarine
2 cups all-purpose flour
Pinch salt

1/2 cup powdered sugar
1 teaspoon vanilla

Preheat oven to 350 degrees. Cream margarine, flour, salt and powdered sugar together; add vanilla, beating well. Pinch off pieces and roll in small 2 inch rolls. Bake on *un*greased cookie sheets for 20 minutes.
While still warm roll in powdered sugar; cool and roll in powdered sugar again.
Makes 4 dozen

Grandma and Grandpa
"G" at their home in
Wilmington, NC.
1994

Marissa's Favorite Lemon Cookies

1 (18.25 ounce) package Duncan Hines Lemon Cake Mix
1 (4 ounce) carton Cool Whip, 1-1/2 cups
1 large egg
1/2 cup powdered sugar

Preheat oven to 350 degrees. Combine the cake mix, Cool Whip and egg together, beating with a spoon until well mixed. Roll into small balls and drop into powdered sugar. Place on greased cookie sheet and bake for 10 to 12 minutes.
 Makes about 3 to 4 dozen.
NOTE: Try these with other cake mixes, (without pudding).

Marissa shares graduation night and her cake with her 3 Grandmothers: Grandma King, Grandma Dee and Grandma Carol.
June 2000

Marissa tries out Modeling!
1998

GRANDMA DEE'S PECAN SANDIES

5 cups all-purpose flour
1 teaspoon baking soda
1 teaspoon cream of tartar
1/4 teaspoon salt
1 cup powdered sugar
1 cup granulated sugar

1 cup butter, softened
1 cup vegetable oil
2 large eggs, beaten
2 teaspoons vanilla
1 cup chopped pecans

Preheat oven to 350 degrees. Mix the flour, baking soda, cream of tartar and salt together; set aside. Mix the powdered sugar, granulated sugar, butter, oil, eggs and vanilla on low speed of electric mixer. Add the flour mixture to creamed mixture and stir in the pecans. Roll in small balls. Place on ungreased cookie sheet. Press each cookie with a glass dipped in sugar. Bake for 10 to 12 minutes. Makes about 80 cookies

SNOWBALLS, MEXICAN WEDDING COOKIE, ETC.

1 cup butter, softened
1/2 cup sifted powdered sugar
2 cups all-purpose flour

2 teaspoons vanilla
2 cups chopped pecans
    finely chopped

Preheat oven to 350 degrees. Cream butter and sugar until smooth & creamy. Blend in flour, vanilla and pecans. Roll in small balls. Bake on ungreased cookie sheet for 7 to 10 minutes. Roll in powdered sugar while still warm. Cool, then roll in powdered sugar again.
Makes 2 to 3 dozen.

Variation: add 1/2 cup flaked coconut to mixture.

GREAT AUNT MAGGIE'S BROWN NUT SUGAR COOKIES

1/2 cup shortening
1 cup light brown sugar
1 large egg
1-1/2 cups all-purpose flour

1/2 teaspoon baking soda
1/4 teaspoon salt
1/2 teaspoon vanilla
3/4 cup pecans, finely
chopped

Preheat oven to 350 degrees. Cream shortening and sugar; add egg and beat well. Combine flour, baking soda and salt; add to creamed mixture. Add vanilla and pecans, mixing well. Mold dough into a roll. Wrap waxed paper and chill in refrigerator. Slice into thin slices and bake on greased cookie sheet for 10 to 12 minutes. Makes about 3-1/2 dozen.

Aunt Maggie turned 100 years old on Feb. 16, 2001. Here she is at her birthday party, holding one of her birthday cards.

BUTTERSCOTCH KRISPIE TREATS

1/2 cup butterscotch pieces
2 tablespoons butter

2-1/2 cups mini marshmallows
2-1/2 cups Rice Krispies cereal

Combine butterscotch pieces and butter in a large microwavable bowl. Cook uncovered 2 minutes at powder control #7 or until melted. Stir in marshmallows. Cook uncovered 2 minutes or until marshmallows are softened, stirring 2 times. Stir until smooth. Stir cereal into mixture & with back of a spoon sprayed with Pam, press into greased 8 inch square dish. Cut into squares.

CHEESECAKE BARS

CRUST:
With a fork, stir together until crumbly:

1 cup all-purpose flour
1/3 cup light brown sugar, firmly packed
1/2 cup finely chopped nuts
1/3 cup melted butter

Remove **1 cup** of mixture and set aside
Press the rest into 8 inch square baking pan.
Bake at 350 degrees for 15 minutes. Remove from oven…..leave oven on.

FILLING:
Beat together with electric mixer:

1 (8 ounce) package cream cheese   **1/4 cup sugar**
1 large egg   **1 tablespoon lemon juice**
2 tablespoons milk   **1 teaspoon vanilla**

Pour over baked crust. Sprinkle reserved topping on top and bake at 350 degrees for 25 minutes. Makes 16, 2 inch squares.

CINNAMON CRUNCH BARS

12 graham cracker squares   **1 cup light brown sugar**
2 cups pecans, chopped   **1/2 teaspoon cinnamon**
1 cup butter

Preheat oven to 400 degrees. In bottom of greased 10x15 inch jelly roll pan, arrange cracker squares in a single layer, touching. Sprinkle chopped pecans evenly over crackers. In a small saucepan combine butter, brown sugar and . cinnamon. Stirring constantly, cook over medium heat until sugar dissolves and mixture begins to boil. Boil for 3 minutes longer <u>without</u> stirring, then pour over crackers. Bake in pre-heated oven for 8 to 10 minutes until bubbly and slight darker around the edges. Cool completely in pan. Break into pieces. Store in airtight container.

GRANDMA DEE'S SUGAR COOKIES

2/3 cup butter
1-1/4 cups sugar
2 large eggs
1-1/2 teaspoons vanilla

2-1/2 cups all-purpose flour
1/2 teaspoon salt
2 teaspoons baking powder

Preheat oven to 350 degrees. Cream butter and sugar together till light and fluffy; add eggs and vanilla, beating well. Sift flour, salt and baking powder together; add to above and mix well. This recipe does not have to chill. Roll out on lightly floured surface and cut into shapes. Place on *un*greased cookie sheets and bake for 10 to 12 minutes. Remove immediately from cookie sheets. Makes about 2 dozen

BROWN SUGAR COOKIES
Granny's "slice 'n' bake"!

1 cup butter, softened
2 cups light brown sugar, packed
2 large eggs
1 teaspoon vanilla

3-1/2 cups plain flour
1 teaspoon baking soda
1/2 teaspoon salt
1 cup chopped pecans

Cream butter, gradually adding brown sugar; cream till light and fluffy. Add eggs and vanilla. Sift together the flour, baking soda and salt; gradually add to creamed mixture. Stir in pecans. Shape into 2, 16 inch rolls; wrap in waxed paper and chill at least 4 hours. Preheat oven to 375 degrees. Cut rolls into 1/2 inch slices. Place on *un*greased cookie sheets and bake for 6 to 8 minutes. Makes about 7 dozen.

Granny's Tip:

Always *pack* brown sugar when measuring. Press firmly into the measuring cup with the back of the spoon and scrape off the top with the back of a knife.

BABY CHEESECAKES
Party favorites!

72 vanilla wafers
3 (8 ounce) packages cream cheese, softened
1 cup sugar
1-1/2 teaspoons vanilla
5 large eggs

Preheat oven to 350 degrees. Line miniature muffin tins with a vanilla wafer, round side down. Beat with cream cheese till all of the lumps are gone. Add sugar, vanilla and eggs. Beat until well mixed. Spoon about 1 tablespoon of the filling over the vanilla wafers. Bake for about 20 minutes.
While these are baking, prepare the topping:

1 pint sour cream
1/4 cup sugar
1 teaspoon vanilla
1 (21 ounce) can cherry pie filling

Stir the sour cream, sugar and vanilla together. Remove cheesecakes from oven and spoon a small amount of topping over each one. Return to oven and bake 5 minutes more. Let cool and refrigerate When ready to serve, put a cherry and a little of the filling on top of each little cheesecake. Makes 6 dozen.

MACAROONS

6 tablespoons all-purpose flour
1-1/2 cups sugar
1 teaspoon salt

4 cups flaked coconut
6 large egg whites, unbeaten
2 teaspoons vanilla

Preheat oven to 325 degrees. Combine flour, sugar and salt; add coconut, egg whites and vanilla. Beat well. Drop by teaspoons onto well-greased and floured cookie sheets. Bake for 15 minutes until edges are just brown. Remove to cake cooling rack immediately to cool and firm. Makes 2-1/2 dozen.

LEMON-COCONUT BARS

In a food processor, pulse to mix: (or sift together)
1 cup all-purpose flour
1/4 cup powdered sugar
Add:
1 stick butter or margarine, in pieces
Pulse about 12 times   (or cut into with pastry cutter)
Pat firmly in ungreased 8 x 8 x 2 inch baking pan.
Bake in preheated 350 degree oven for 15 minutes.
Leave oven on.
Meanwhile:
In a medium bowl, beat:
3 large eggs
Sift together and add to eggs:
2 tablespoons all-purpose flour
1/2 teaspoon baking powder
1/8 teaspoon salt
1 cup granulated sugar
Add:
2 tablespoons lemon juice
Whisk till smooth, then stir in:
1 cup flaked coconut, breaking up any lumps
Pour over baked crust and with rubber spatula, _gently_ distribute
coconut evenly.
Return to oven and bake for 20 to 25 minutes more.
While still warm, pour icing (below) over _OR_ let cool and sift powdered sugar over top. Let cool completely and cut into squares
or bars. ───────────────
NOTE: It cuts better if refrigerated for a while after cooling.

ICING:
Mix together and spread evenly over bars before cutting:
1 cup sifted powdered sugar
1 tablespoon lemon juice
1 teaspoon coconut extract

TEA CAKES

Children used to carry these in their pockets while playing. When they got hungry during the day, they just reached in their pocket, for a big round teacake cookie, took a bite and kept on playing.

1 cup butter-flavored Crisco
1-1/2 cups sugar
1 teaspoon baking soda
1/2 cup buttermilk
3 large eggs

1 teaspoon vanilla
4 cups all-purpose flour
2 teaspoons baking powder
1/2 teaspoon salt
2 teaspoons nutmeg

Preheat oven to 400 degrees. Cream shortening and sugar. Dissolve baking soda in buttermilk and add to creamed mixture. Add eggs and vanilla. Sift flour, baking powder, salt and nutmeg together and add to creamed mixture. Roll out on lightly floured cloth or board and cut out with a large round cookie cutter. Grandma used a glass dipped in flour (to keep glass from getting sticky). Bake on *un*greased baking sheets about 8 minutes. Do not let them get brown. Makes about 3 dozen.

CAKE MIX COOKIES

1 (18.25 ounce) package cake mix, any flavor
1/4 cup sugar
2 large eggs
1/2 cup vegetable oil
1/4 cup pecans, chopped

Preheat oven to 350 degrees. Mix all of the above ingredients together. Drop by heaping teaspoonfuls on *un*greased cookie sheets, 2 inches apart. Bake for about 10 minutes.
Makes about 6 dozen.

BABY RUTH BARS

4 cups Rice Krispy cereal
1-1/2 cups cream style peanut butter
1 cup light corn syrup
1 cup white sugar
1 (6 ounce) package chocolate chips
1 (6 ounce) package butterscotch chips

Put the cereal and peanut butter in a large bowl and set aside.
Put the corn syrup and sugar together in a large boiler and bring
to a boil. Pour hot syrup over peanut butter/Krispy mixture and
mix well with a spoon. Spread and press into 9x13 pan.
Melt chocolate chips and butterscotch chips together in top of
double boiler or over low heat. Spread over Krispy mixture like
frosting. Let cool and cut into bars. Makes 24 bar cookies.

GRANDMA DEE'S SOFT OATMEAL COOKIES

1 cup shortening
3/4 cup white sugar
3/4 cup light brown sugar
2 large eggs
2 tablespoons molasses
1-3/4 cups plain flour

1 teaspoon salt
1 teaspoon baking soda
1 teaspoon cinnamon
2 cups quick cooking oats
1 cup raisins

Preheat oven to 350 degrees. Cream shortening and sugars together; add eggs and molasses. Sift the dry ingredients together
and add to creamed mixture. Stir in oats and raisins. Drop by
teaspoons onto greased cookie sheets and bake at 350 degrees
for about 12 minutes. They should look slightly undercooked in
center. They will firm up as they cool on wire rack. This makes
them chewy. If you want a crisp cookie, bake slightly longer, about
15 minutes. Makes about 45 cookies.

Honor YOUR Grandma in one of our future Granny Cookbooks!

We just bet that some of your fondest childhood memories revolve around your Grandma's kitchen; baking cookies together, wearing one of her aprons, listening to her stories about *her* memories, licking the beaters & bowl. Did she teach you how to make *biscuits?* Did she go to your Christmas pageant, make paper chains and string popcorn with you to trim the tree? Did you go out into the woods and choose the Christmas tree together?

I'm sure you have many charming stories about your Grandma and we'd love to hear from you. Be sure and include one of her recipes and if possible, a clear picture of her, which, of course, we'll return. Include your name, address & phone number. If we feature your Granny in one of our future Granny Cookbooks, we'll send you a complimentary copy.

Please send entries to:

Miss Dee's Kitchen
P. O. Box 3332
Boone, North Carolina, 28607

INDEX

GRANNY'S KITCHEN ARITHMETIC

MAIN DISHES

SOUPS

VEGETABLES

Granny Says:
Put your favorite
recipes here:

RECIPE   PAGE

NOTES